SELF-IDENTITY AND PERSONAL AUTONOMY

We are all persons or selves. But what exactly does it mean that we possess an identity and autonomy as persons or selves? This book explores the closely related problems of self-identity and personal autonomy within the framework of contemporary analytical anthropology, a blend of analytical philosophy of mind and action with moral psychology. Cuypers first critically examines the empiricist bundle theory and metaphysical ego theory of self-identity as well as the hierarchical Frankfurt/Dworkin model of personal autonomy. Arguing that all these standard views are found wanting, Cuypers then offers an alternative 'personalist' theory of personal identity, plus an innovative 'moderately heteronomous' theory of autonomy without ever going beyond the analytical frame of reference.

In critical discussion with analytical philosophers such as Derek Parfit, John Perry and Harry Frankfurt the author develops an original perspective on the nature of persons or selves that is orthogonal to the received views in analytical anthropology.

ASHGATE NEW CRITICAL THINKING
IN PHILOSOPHY

The *Ashgate New Critical Thinking in Philosophy* series aims to bring high quality research monograph publishing back into focus for authors, the international library market, and student, academic and research readers. Headed by an international editorial advisory board of acclaimed scholars from across the philosophical spectrum, this new monograph series presents cutting-edge research from established as well as exciting new authors in the field; spans the breadth of philosophy and related disciplinary and interdisciplinary perspectives; and takes contemporary philosophical research into new directions and debate.

Series Editorial Board:

Self-Identity and Personal Autonomy

An analytical anthropology

STEFAAN E. CUYPERS
Catholic University of Leuven, Belgium (Flanders)

Routledge
Taylor & Francis Group

LONDON AND NEW YORK

First published 2001 by Ashgate Publishing

Reissued 2018 by Routledge
2 Park Square, Milton Park, Abingdon, Oxon OX14 4RN
711 Third Avenue, New York, NY 10017, USA

Routledge is an imprint of the Taylor & Francis Group, an informa business

Publisher's Note
The publisher has gone to great lengths to ensure the quality of this reprint but points out that some imperfections in the original copies may be apparent.

Disclaimer
The publisher has made every effort to trace copyright holders and welcomes correspondence from those they have been unable to contact.

A Library of Congress record exists under LC control number: 2001027832

ISBN 13: 978-1-138-63425-1 (hbk)
ISBN 13: 978-0-415-79277-6 (pbk)
ISBN 13: 978-1-315-21142-8 (ebk)

Contents

Preface   *vii*

Acknowledgements   *ix*

Introduction: Analytical Anthropology   1

PART I: SELF-IDENTITY   13

1   The Problem of Personal Identity   15

2   Parfit's and Perry's Impersonal Solution   37

3   Atomistic Self-Identity and Analytical Personalism   57

PART II: PERSONAL AUTONOMY   83

4   Hierarchical Autonomy, Self-Identification and Self-Evaluation   85

5   Frankfurt on the Nature of the Will   107

6   Community and Authenticity of the Self   131

Appendix: The Memory Theory of Personal Identity   151

Bibliography   161

Index of Names   171

Preface

One of the big issues in philosophy is the perplexity and puzzle of our own existence. Addressing the question 'Who am I?' amounts to the same thing as taking up the philosophical questions about our own identity and autonomy as persons or selves. In this book I tackle this issue by setting forth and explaining my views on the closely related problems of self-identity and personal autonomy. I defend a *personalist* theory of personal identity and a *moderately heteronomous* theory of autonomy within the framework of contemporary research in analytical philosophy of mind and action and analytical moral psychology, which I dub 'analytical anthropology' for reasons set out in the introductory chapter.

In the first part, with regard to the problem of self-identity, I claim that there is something deeply wrong with the standard debate between materialist empiricists and dualist metaphysicians about personal identity through time. In light of our common sense and scientific beliefs about the world and our ordinary practical values, neither the empiricist approach nor the metaphysical approach can adequately account for both the ontology of personal identity and the importance of personal identity in practical contexts which involve responsibility, love, prudential self-interest and the like. After introducing the problem as I see it (chapter one) and critically discussing the influential impersonal solution of Parfit and Perry (chapter two), I outline a third, innovative theoretical approach — which I call 'analytical personalism' — to the problem, pointing towards a satisfactory theory both of the nature and the importance of personal identity (chapter three).

In the second part, with regard to the problem of personal autonomy, I claim that the influential hierarchical or 'Frankfurt/Dworkin' model of personal autonomy is fundamentally mistaken about its two cornerstones: self-identification and self-evaluation (chapter four). After presenting the model, I critically argue that the process of self-identification cannot entirely be rooted in autonomous 'acts of the will', and, furthermore, that the process of self-evaluation depends in an important sense on the normative impact of other people's attitudes. As an innovative alternative I then sketch a view of personal autonomy in terms of 'passive' self-identification on the basis of volitional necessity (chapter five) and in terms of 'social' self-evaluation based on recognition by others (chapter six). I call this view 'moderately heteronomous' because it incorporates 'alienating influences' in its heart without becoming totally uncontrollable. Although passivity and social dependence are commonly treated as incompatible with autonomy, I maintain that both volitional necessity and other-directedness are constitutive of authentic personal autonomy.

Acknowledgements

Parts of the following previously published articles of mine appear either verbatim or modified in the book: 'Is Personal Autonomy the First Principle of Education?', *Journal of Philosophy of Education* 26 (1992), pp. 5-17; 'What Wittgenstein Would Have Said About Personal Autonomy', *Studies in Philosophy and Education* 14 (1995), pp. 251-265, with kind permission from Kluwer Academic Publishers; 'Harry Frankfurt on the Will, Autonomy and Necessity', *Ethical Perspectives* 5 (1998), pp. 44-52; and 'Philosophical Atomism and the Metaphysics of Personal Identity', *International Philosophical Quarterly* XXXVIII (1998), pp. 349-368. I am grateful to the editors and publishers for their permission to use material from these articles.

I am also grateful to the *Onderzoeksraad* of the Catholic University of Leuven, Belgium (Flanders) for financial support.

I am indebted to Dale Kidd and 'Typeface' for the production of the final camera-ready copy of the manuscript.

I owe a special debt to my initial mentors at the Institute of Philosophy, Arnold Burms and Herman De Dijn who first introduced me to 'analytical anthropology' and to Paul Smeyers who first stimulated me to write about it in English.

Finally, I would like to express my deepest gratitude to Ann my wife for everything. I dedicate the book to her and our daughters Paulien and Marjan.

S.E.C.
Institute of Philosophy, Leuven
January 2001

Introduction

Analytical Anthropology

According to the most general common sense classification of the elements in the universe, there are things, plants, animals, and persons, perhaps even divine ones. You and I are human persons. But what exactly does it mean that we have an identity and autonomy as a person or a self? What is a person or a human being? To this question different intellectual traditions give different answers. The theoretical questioning of man by man gives rise to different kinds of *anthropologies* (from the Greek 'anthropos', meaning *man*). My line of attacking the questions of self-identity and personal autonomy is not only *philosophical*, but also, within the field of philosophy, *analytical*. I call this approach 'analytical anthropology'. Such an anthropology is thus a philosophical anthropology in the analytical style of philosophizing.

Analytical anthropology as a philosophical specialty is different from scientific cultural anthropology, and as an analytical specialty it is different form continental anthropology, i.e., philosophical anthropology in the continental style of doing philosophy. Before delineating further in this introductory chapter the nature of analytical anthropology as both philosophical and analytical, I draw attention to the new label 'analytical anthropology' itself. It covers the same area of expertise as the label 'analytical philosophy of man', which is, however, not gender-sensitive.* Analytical anthropology comprises in a way both analytical *philosophy of mind and action* and analytical *moral psychology*, but only in so far as these domains have something to say about the nature of the human person. I think it is to the advantage of analytical philosophy to have a non-sexist label for this cross-section. Analytical philosophy is after all not solely logic, epistemology, philosophy of science and philosophy of language, though these domains are, and always will be, dominant in the analytical tradition. To my mind, analytical philosophy has some important things to say about our identity and autonomy as persons or selves.

---

* Throughout this book personal pronouns are used in the generic rather than in any gendered sense.

1

Philosophy as contemplation and argumentation

As indicated, analytical anthropology must be distinguished not only from philosophical anthropologies in the continental style of philosophizing — such as Heidegger's analysis of *Dasein* (Heidegger, 1927) — but also from scientific anthropologies. Just as philosophy must be distinguished from science, analytical anthropology must be clearly distinguished from anthropologies in the social sciences which comprise sociology, economics, political science, history, psychology and cultural anthropology. In what sense then is analytical anthropology not a scientific but a *philosophical* discipline? This question, of course, amounts to a question about the very nature of philosophy. What is philosophy? In my opinion, philosophy is contemplation as well as argumentation. Let me explain this.

What is philosophy all about? Ultimately, philosophy tries to construct a *contemplative image* of man and reality. Philosophy's aim is not the scientific knowledge (or technical manipulation) of reality, nor a literary re-creation of reality, but a reflexive description of reality. Philosophy essentially aims at the ideal of contemplation. Philosophy describes reality with a view to contemplation, while science explains reality with a view to operationalization. Scientific explanation aims at prediction and manipulation: the endpoint of science lies in technology. In other words, science strives less for theoretical insight than for practical utility. Philosophy on the other hand wants to bring about a *unity* and a *whole* by means of a contemplative image. It wants to introduce unity and wholeness into the diversity of knowledge and the confusion of experience in order to bring fragmented thinking and restless life to rest, in contemplation.

This philosophical desire for a contemplative whole is irrevocably linked with the existential meaning of life itself, and is rooted in the interest of the 'metaphysical animal' to give meaning to it all. Contemplation suggests an ultimate and definitive standpoint that is raised above the restlessness of existence and its vicissitudes. But the contemplative ideal of philosophy is, and always will remain, an *ideal*. The fulfilment of the philosophical desire for unity and rest — if it is fulfilled at all — is short-lived and transitory in nature. The contemplative moment is fleeting: '... there is no *vita contemplativa*; there are only moments of contemplative activity abstracted and rescued from the flow of curiosity and contrivance.' (Oakeshott, 1959, p. 541)

Of course, philosophy also has to do with *argumentation*. From a methodological viewpoint, philosophy is even primarily about rational argument (and other formally logical techniques). Despite the clear differences between philosophy and science, the philosophical method of proceeding bears a strong similarity with scientific theory formation. Philosophical procedure — thesis, argument and counter-argument — and scientific procedure — hypothesis, verification and falsification — are closely related in a structural sense. The fact that philosophy operates more conceptually (a priori) and science more empirically (a posteriori) does not affect their formal similarity on the methodological level.

Yet philosophical argumentation still remains subordinated to the philosophical construction of a contemplative image. Rational argument in philosophy is not an end in itself but a *means* of attaining the real end — contemplation. This does not mean, however, that the argumentative method is a negligible aspect of philosophical reflection. On the contrary, the philosophical journey towards contemplation must necessarily pass through the detour of argumentation. The contemplative ideal cannot be pursued directly. Moreover, the success of the philosophical enterprise is never guaranteed. The contemplative moment is not so much an essential end-product as an accidental by-product of philosophy's argumentative method. In his reflections, the philosopher tries to arrive at a contemplative image — the whole — by way of the procedure of argumentation — the parts:

> ... to the extent that there is *one* picture to be grasped reflectively as a whole, the unity of the reflective vision is a task rather than an initial datum. The search for this unity at the reflective level is therefore more appropriately compared to the contemplation of a large and complex painting which is not seen as a unity without a prior exploration of its parts. (Sellars, 1962, p. 4)

So if there is some truth in my view of the nature of philosophy, then philosophical anthropology as a *philosophical* enterprise strives to construct a contemplative image of our self-identity and personal autonomy by way of argumentation.

Distinction with continental anthropology

Analytical anthropology is not only a philosophical specialty, but also, within the field of philosophy, an *analytical* specialty. This characterization raises the question of the nature of analytical philosophy. What is analytical philosophy? Just as there exists a demarcation between philosophy, science and literature (poetry), I think there also exists a demarcation between contemporary analytical and continental philosophy (Biletzki and Matar, 1998; Sim, 2000). Analytical philosophy can be roughly distinguished from continental philosophy in the sense that the analytical style of philosophizing generally includes references to British empiricism (Hobbes, Locke, Berkeley and Hume) while the continental style of philosophy generally contains references to German idealism (the transcendental project of Kant, Fichte, Schelling and Hegel). The analytical style of philosophy is prominent in Great Britain, the United States and Australia, whereas the continental style is more prominent in France and Germany. If philosophy finds itself between the extremes of science and literature, then analytical philosophy seems to be closer to the side of science while continental philosophy seems to be closer to the side of literature.

My demarcation is, however, ideal-typical. 'Analytical' and 'continental' philosophy are in fact labels that apply to various contents. Analytical philosophy can stand for the formal, logical analysis of, for example, Russell but it can also stand for the informal, conceptual analysis of Ryle. My analytical anthropology subscribes to this latter kind of analysis. Continental philosophy can stand for the phenomenology of, for example, Husserl and Merleau-Ponty, the existentialism of Heidegger and Sartre, the structuralism of Barthes and Foucault, the psychoanalysis of Lacan and Irigaray, the hermeneutics of Gadamer and Ricoeur, the critical theory of Benjamin and Habermas and the postmodern deconstructionism of Derrida and Lyotard (McNeill and Feldman, 1998). This division of philosophy into two camps is perhaps not very meaningful, and a gradual distinction between 'more or less' analytical philosophies might be less misleading (Føllesdal, 1996). Husserl, Merleau-Ponty and Sartre, for instance, would then be analytical philosophers to a high degree, but Heidegger and Derrida would not be analytical philosophers, not even to some degree, since they are clearly not at all analytical. For simplicity's sake, in what follows I shall continue to use the ideal-typical distinction between analytical philosophy — i.e., fully analytical philosophers such as Russell — and continental philosophy — i.e., philosophers who are considerably less or not at all analytical. This ideal-typical difference is primarily a matter of style and method.

Analytical philosophy aims directly at explanation and insight. Its leading method is a rational analysis in terms of necessary and sufficient conditions, and the introduction of distinctions to clear up ambiguities. What is unique to analytical philosophy is its literal and argumentative procedure, as well as its striving for clarity, precision and rational justification. The belief in philosophical progress and the search for truth are central intellectual virtues — even in these postmodern times. Analytical philosophy can, in this sense, be seen as a continuation of the classical philosophical project, begun by Plato and Aristotle, which strives for intelligibility and presence.

Continental philosophy on the other hand — at least in its 'less analytical' forms — aims directly at deconstructive critique and evocation, sometimes even provocation. Influenced by the *philosophes du soupçon* — Marx, Nietzsche and Freud — there is clearly a degree of suspicion with regard to the power of reason. Ambiguity is not so much an obstacle to philosophical depth as a vehicle for associative reflection. The use of vague and broad categories, rhetoric and metaphor, and ideologically laden strategies is not curbed but rather encouraged, in the belief that everything is fundamentally a 'text' and radically 'contextual'. Because of its fusion with literature (poetry) and ideology, continental philosophy — or at least a crucial part of it — can in this sense be seen as the end of the classical philosophical project.

The distinction between these two ideal-typical styles of doing philosophy can also be illuminated with the help of my view that philosophy is essentially contemplation (through argumentation). To exaggerate a bit, one could say that continental philosophy aims more directly at the contemplative ideal whereas analytical philosophy aims at this ideal indirectly at best. The metaphysical search for 'the meaning of life' is never or rarely thematized in analytical philosophy (exceptions to this rule are Nagel, 1979; Nozick, 1981, pp. 571-647), while continental philosophy examines these existential themes more explicitly. Or at least one can say that continental philosophy — particularly the postmodern philosophy of difference espoused by, say, Derrida and Lyotard — is characterized by a highly problematic relation to the ideal of contemplation and presence. Continental philosophy, specifically postmodern deconstructionism, seems well aware of the impossibility of the project of the classical philosophy of presence and thus of the end of philosophy as such. Now, to come to my point, in relation to the philosophical ideal of contemplation and the metaphysical meaning of life, I think that analytical philosophy can helpfully be characterized as *'cool and thin'* and continental philosophy as *'hot and thick'*.

Continental philosophy focuses its attention, first and foremost, on facts and meanings that are related to existential, religious or moral attitudes. It begins with an experience that goes together with an existential attitude to life, such as *Geworfenheit* in Heidegger, or an encounter that hangs together with a moral attitude, such as *le visage de l'Autre* in Levinas. In this sense hot and thick issues are fundamental to continental philosophy. Analytical philosophy, on the other hand, is not guided by the experience of meaning(lessness) or the metaphysical search for the meaning of life. Analytical philosophers generally adopt a neutral position and devote their attention to consolidated problems, such as the ontological problem of universals and the epistemological problem of the justification of belief. These issues do not seem to have any existential relevance, at least not directly. In this sense cool and thin topics are central to analytical philosophy.

5

As a result of this, in the continental tradition one can find thick images of man and world, for instance Hegel's metaphysical ontology (reality is the dialectical self-realization of Absolute Spirit) and the metaphysical anthropologies of Marx (man is praxis), Nietzsche (man is will to power) and Freud (man is sexual desire). In postmodern continental philosophy, such contemplative images are still present, but more as objects of re-interpretation, critique or deconstruction. Though a thick image of man and reality in continental philosophy is the prototype of a contemplative image, in a certain sense analytical philosophy also pursues the contemplative ideal. Yet in the analytical tradition one finds, at most, thin images of man and world, with which I will instantly associate Wittgensteinian *perspicuous representations*. So continental philosophy seeks a hot contemplative image of man and reality, whereas analytical philosophy seems to be satisfied with a cool contemplative image, or even with much less.

As the subtitle of this book indicates, my personal preference is a philosophical anthropology in the analytical style of doing philosophy. Compared with continental philosophy, the value of an analytical anthropology lies in the clarity of its style and in the precisely articulated and rationally argued view that it provides. This is not the place to argue meticulously for the superiority of analytical anthropology. Suffice it to say that in light of the classical, Platonic and Aristotelian philosophical project which strives for intelligibility and presence, I believe that my personal preference for an analytical anthropology requires no further apology.

Perspicuous representation or descriptive metaphysics

In the words of Ludwig Wittgenstein, analytical philosophy tries to be, at most, a perspicuous representation (*übersichtliche Darstellung*):

> A main source of our failure to understand is that we do not *command a clear view* of the use of our words. — Our grammar is lacking in this sort of perspicuity. A perspicuous representation produces just that understanding which consists in 'seeing connexions'. Hence the importance of finding and inventing *intermediate cases*. The concept of a perspicuous representation is of fundamental significance to us. It earmarks the form of account we give, the way we look at things. (Is this a 'Weltanschauung'?) (Wittgenstein, 1953, I, § 122)

A perspicuous representation of the conceptual field surrounding the concept of a person or a self — the topic of this book — is then a rather *cool and thin picture* which is closely related to the common sense view. Although a perspicuous representation, like the one aimed at in this book, does not rest on a hot and thick metaphysical insight, it nevertheless preserves the aspects of unity and wholeness. Philosophical interest in a perspicuous representation is awakened first of all by its aspects of unity and wholeness, aspects which form an essential part of the contemplative ideal. In this cool and thin sense, the project of constructing a perspicuous representation is still strongly linked to the contemplative ideal.

To put it another way, the philosophical project of constructing a perspicuous representation is the project of philosophically describing our conceptual scheme and its parts. According to Peter Strawson, the foremost task of analytical philosophy lies in the construction of such a descriptive metaphysics:

> ... to establish the connections between the major structural features or elements of our conceptual scheme — to exhibit it, not as a rigidly deductive system, but as a coherent whole whose parts are mutually supportive and mutually dependent, interlocking in an intelligible way — to do this may well seem ... the proper, or at least the major, task of analytical philosophy. (Strawson, 1985, p. 23)

My analytical anthropology in this book forms part of this philosophical project of constructing a descriptive metaphysics. In other words, an analytical anthropology, as I construe it, is a descriptive metaphysics of the person. In a certain sense, this means that analytical anthropology is then not strictly analytical, since it is not exclusively concerned with a conceptual analysis of the conceptual field surrounding the concept of the person or the self. My analytical anthropology does not offer an answer to the question: what are the necessary and sufficient conditions for self-identity and personal autonomy? Conceptual clarity — however indispensable — is not enough. The method of conceptual analysis, just like the argumentative method, serves the construction of a contemplative image. The ultimate goal of a descriptive metaphysics of the person — contemplative unity and wholeness — can only be attained at the level of a *conceptual synthesis* or a perspicuous representation.

However, not every philosopher in the Anglo-American analytical tradition will agree with the description of analytical philosophy's task as the construction of a perspicuous representation or a descriptive metaphysics. On the contrary, the current orthodoxy in analytical philosophy rejects the contemplative ideal — even in its cool and thin sense — and adheres to the *scientific* ideal. Influenced by logical positivism and scientism, contemporary analytical philosophy sees itself primarily as a *naturalized* philosophy, i.e., as a philosophy that is directly connected to the natural sciences and the brain and behavioural sciences (Churchland, 1986). Since the beginning of the 1960s, the philosophical description — the perspicuous representation — of ordinary language philosophy has increasingly given way to the philosophical theory of naturalized philosophy. This is apparent, for instance, with naturalized epistemology, and with the fusion of philosophical psychology and semantics with cognitive psychology, linguistics, computer science and neuroscience to form cognitive science, bringing about a naturalization of these philosophical disciplines. In this form, analytical philosophy is in line with the empirical sciences and its method differs very little, if at all, from scientific method. Just like strictly scientific theories, philosophical theories also contain hypotheses, thought experiments, laws and explanations. While analytical philosophy in its naturalized form cannot carry out a quantitative study of typically philosophical topics such as meaning and intentionality, it nonetheless tries to approximate the scientific ideal as closely as possible.

In light of the idea of philosophy as essentially contemplation (via argumentation), the analytical style of philosophizing moves between the two extremes of a perspicuous representation, on the one hand, and a scientific theory, on the other — between the extremes of descriptive metaphysics and naturalized philosophy. The further analytical philosophy moves away from the contemplative ideal, even in its thin and cool sense, the closer it gets to the scientific ideal, and vice versa. My analytical anthropology is situated at the pole of descriptive metaphysics, close to the contemplative ideal. In this book, I attempt to provide a perspicuous representation of two central aspects of human existence: a person's self-identity and autonomy. Though at times I will be quite argumentative, the final result is still — for me at least — a certain sort of contemplative image of man in the cool and thin sense.

Self-identity and personal autonomy

My perspicuous representation of a person's self-identity and autonomy in this book constitutes only a *partial* analytical anthropology. Other significant aspects of human existence — e.g., personhood, the relation between mind and body, intentional action and practical reasoning — are scarcely dealt with. However, I think that self-identity and personal autonomy are two *central* aspects whose philosophical profiles are sufficiently sharp and perspicuously represented in this book to evoke a contemplative image of what it means to live as a person, albeit only in a cool and thin sense. Let me

8

now give an overview of my philosophical anthropology.

The first three chapters deal with the issue of self-identity. In chapter one I introduce the problem of personal identity as discussed in contemporary analytical philosophy. I then argue that this standard debate between *empiricists* and *metaphysicians* leads to an aporetic conclusion. Neither the bundle theory — defended by, among others, Anthony Quinton and Sydney Shoemaker — nor the ego theory — defended by, among others, Roderick Chisholm and Richard Swinburne — can adequately account for both the nature and the importance of personal identity. On the empiricist account, the importance of personal identity reduces to a practical fiction, while, on the metaphysical account, the nature of personal identity evaporates into an ontological fiction. Correspondingly, the empiricist bundle theory espouses a destructive conventionalism, whereas the metaphysical ego theory embraces a miraculous essentialism. In the light of our common sense intuitions about practical values as well as scientific beliefs about the make-up of reality, the analytical problem of personal identity, therefore, still remains unresolved.

In chapter two I critically discuss Derek Parfit's and John Perry's *impersonal* solution to the problem of personal identity. According to this radically reductionist solution, personal identity consists in nothing but mental connectedness and continuity, and these relations can completely be described in impersonal terms. This bold empiricist view is presented in the course of discussing the thought experiments of the spectrum and reduplication. Parfit's and Perry's influential impersonal solution has, however, extremely revisionist consequences for practical matters such as responsibility, love and prudential self-interest. I then argue that their solution is unsatisfactory because impersonalism and revisionism causes not only a radical distortion of the personalist descriptive metaphysics but also a full destruction of the personalist moral and emotional reactive attitudes of every man of common sense.

In chapter three I offer my *analytical personalism* as an alternative for the bundle theory (or its impersonal variant) as well as the ego theory of personal identity, both of which I interpret as atomistic views. Since I have no ambition to directly solve the problem of personal identity in this book, I limit myself to the task of sketching a general framework to diagnose what is wrong with the standard debate and to suggest its therapy. One atomistic virus that I eradicate is the perceptual model of introspective self-knowledge. The crucial shift from the atomistic self as a private object to the person as a public agent is made with the aid of Peter Strawson's personalist descriptive metaphysics which contains the essential preliminaries for an alternative solution to the problem of personal identity. I then briefly outline

9

how such a Strawsonian non-atomistic view can be developed further into an alternative view of personal identity that can adequately account for both the nature and the importance of personal identity. This resultant analytical personalism comprises bodily identity, agential identity and narrative identity as the essential building blocks for personal identity.

The theme of the next three chapters is personal autonomy. In chapter four I critically discuss the main tenets of the hierarchical model of Harry Frankfurt and Gerald Dworkin and introduce my *moderately heteronomous* theory of personal autonomy. I criticize the notions of self-identification and self-evaluation which are of the utmost importance to this model. Instead of relying on such 'acts of the will' as decision and choice for the explanation of self-identification and self-evaluation, I stress the non-voluntaristic as well as the non-individualistic character of these processes and analyze them in terms of volitional necessity and social dependence. As a consequence of my criticism, the concept of caring about oneself substitutes for the concept of extreme personal autonomy. In my moderately heteronomous theory, then, two elements, passive self-identification and social self-evaluation, come together in the concept of a person who cares about himself. Accordingly, the stability of personal autonomy is exchanged for the fragility of caring about oneself.

In chapter five I develop further the first half of my moderately heteronomous theory of personal autonomy, i.e. my *passive* view of self-identification. To that end, I give an interpretation of Harry Frankfurt's complex theory of the will. I introduce and justify a clarifying tripartite distinction: the appetitive will (desires), the active will (decisions), and the substantial will (carings). Now both the first and the second conception of the will have their natural home in the debate on freedom and determinism between compatibilists and incompatibilists. The third conception, however, transcends the boundaries of this traditional debate because the autonomy of the will as caring is not only compatible with deterministic necessity, it also positively requires volitional necessity. The constitution and autonomy of the substantial will needs the necessities of the will. Although this last conception of the will is somewhat unfamiliar and non-standard in the debate, I argue that it seizes the all-important basic structure of our volitional nature. In view of the tripartite distinction I then shall show how my moderately heteronomous theory of personal identity can partly be explicated as the combination of a hybrid thesis about the concept of personal autonomy with an asymmetrical dependency thesis, according to which active self-identification depends upon passive self-identification, but not vice versa.

In chapter six I develop further the second half of my moderately heteronomous theory of personal autonomy, i.e. my *community* view of self-evaluation. For that purpose, I construct a community view of the authenticity of the self by using Wittgensteinian ideas. Although Wittgenstein himself never explored these existential themes head-on in his own work, it is possible to construct a Wittgensteinian outlook on the nature and importance of personal autonomy. My construction and defence of such a community view is based on Charles Taylor's moral psychology. The main conclusion I draw from such an applied Wittgensteinian philosophy is that the ideal of autonomy as authenticity substitutes for the ideal of autonomy as radical self-determination. I argue that the necessary possibility conditions for such an ideal of authenticity are recognition by other people (social dependence) and horizons of significance (forms of life) in a community. My community view, however, is subtly distinct from the view of contemporary communitarianism and feminism about authentic personal autonomy.

PART I
SELF-IDENTITY

Chapter One

The Problem of Personal Identity

Introduction

Since Heraclitus remarked that no one can step twice into the same river, philosophers have wrestled with the identity of things and, in particular, with personal identity. How can someone possibly remain one and the same person throughout the course of their life, given their physical and mental changes? This old philosophical question has led to a controversy in contemporary analytical philosophy that continues a discussion from the classical rationalism and empiricism of the 17th and 18th centuries (Martin and Barresi, 2000).

In this chapter, following a short history of the concept of the person and a more detailed description of the analytical problem of personal identity, I shall present and critically evaluate two prominent analytical theories of personal identity: the *empiricist* bundle theory and the *metaphysical* ego theory. The proponents of the former theory — notably Quinton, Shoemaker and Parfit — are rooted in the tradition of John Locke and David Hume, while the proponents of the latter theory — notably Chisholm, Swinburne and Madell — are rooted in the tradition of René Descartes, Joseph Butler and Thomas Reid. The basis of my critical evaluation of both the empiricist and the metaphysical solution to the roblem of personal identity lies in the *common sense* conceptions of the phenomenon of personal identity. In light of these common sense conceptions, I shall then attempt to demonstrate that the standard debate between empiricists and metaphysicians about personal identity in analytical philosophy culminates in an aporia.

I restrict myself here to the *standard* debate between the adherents of the two most prominent theories. This restriction means that various non-standard theories will *not* be discussed.[1] The underlying reason for this restric-

---

1. For an excellent introduction to *the state of the art* of the standard debate, see Shoemaker and Swinburne, 1984. Also very helpful are Perry, 1975a, Oksenberg Rorty, 1976 and Noonan, 1989. Among the non-standard theories of personal identity in contemporary analytical philosophy, one could mention the *body* theory put forward by Williams, 1973, pp. 1-81 and the *brain* theory put forward by Mackie, 1976, pp. 173-203 and by Nagel, 1986, pp. 43-45.

tion is my belief that the non-standard theories either do not provide a clear alternative to the bundle theory or the ego theory, or else they can in some sense be reduced to one of these two.

The history of the concept of the person

In contemporary analytical philosophy, the concept of the person is most often analyzed in terms of the concept of the *self.* This identification of person with self is not a necessary one, but a contingent result of the conceptual development that reflects the history of the West. In his essay entitled *Une Catégorie de l'Esprit Humain: la Notion de Personne, Celle de 'Moi'*, the renowned French anthropologist Marcel Mauss (1938) outlines the historical development of the concept of the person, resulting in its fusing with the concept of the self.[2] He distinguishes four stages of development.

Originally the notion of the person had the same content as the notion of *mask* in cultural anthropology. Though the etymology is dubious, the Latin word *persona* is said to be derived from *per-sonare*: through (*per*) the mask one hears (*sonare*) the voice of the masked one. Additionally, *persona* is presumed to derive from the Etruscan *phersu* and to be related to the Greek *prosopon* — both words meaning, among other things, 'mask'. This mythical idea of person as mask was not only an element of ancient Greek and Latin culture, but is still present today in so-called primitive cultures. In these strongly ritualized forms of society, the identity of a member of the community is fully determined by the role that he or she plays in a collective drama. By inherited names and titles, one is identified with one's ancestors from a mythical past. The identity of a tribal member is purely a function of the social place he or she occupies within the continuity of the tribe. The external mask gives the person a fixed and recognizable profile — the person as mask is a character.

In ancient Rome — Mauss's second stage — the idea of the person acquired a more limited social content and came to signify the equivalent of *legal person.* Nowadays we are familiar not only with natural, but also with artificial legal persons such as corporations and societies. This juridical concept implies that the person is a subject of rights and duties in the public sphere. Within the legal order, there are only persons (*personae*), property or things (*res*) and actions (*actiones*). Roman law granted citizenship to every free Roman man, thus distinguishing him as a responsible individual from barbarians and slaves (*servus non habet personam*). Contrary to these non-persons, the Roman citizen had the right to a surname, a first name and a

---

2. For the English translation of, and additional commentary on, this famous essay, see Carrithers, Collins and Lukes, 1985.

pseudonym (nickname), which guaranteed his recognition as a prominent dignitary. Outside the social and legal order, the respectable status of the individual disappeared; the Roman legal person was a public figure.

Influenced by Stoicism and Christianity, the idea of the person underwent another shift of meaning. In this third stage, the juridical concept of the person gradually expanded to include the ethical and theological concept of *moral substance*. It was mainly the Stoics who introduced the ideas of moral self-consciousness and ethical autonomy, while the Christians elaborated the religious idea that all people are one in Christ without distinction. The title of person was no longer dependent on a particular social or legal order, but acquired an additional individualistic and universalistic foundation. Individual conscience and the universal dignity of the person were ultimately founded by the medieval moral and religious worldview. The onto-theological disputes concerning the trinity of God the Father, the Son and the Holy Spirit — three persons in one substance — had repercussions not only on the conception of the divine nature but also on the conception of human nature. *Persona — rationalis naturae individua substantia*, according to Boethius's classical medieval definition. It was this Christian articulation of the concept of the person that was to exercise such influence on the self-conception of Western man: the moral person is an internalized individuality.

Finally, philosophy's emancipation from theology and the rise of modern science in the Renaissance announces the fourth stage. The idea of the person was detached not just from the social context but also from the moral and religious context. Moreover, corporeality was considered to be a negligible aspect of personhood. During the Enlightenment (17th and 18th centuries), the concept of the person was fully equated with the psychological concept of the *self* (or with a transcendental variant of the same concept). Particularly under the influence of Protestantism, personhood became exclusively aligned with consciousness of self and self-knowledge. In philosophy, subjectivity became the fundamental principle on which not only epistemology, but also ontology and ethics were based. Descartes's *cogito ergo sum* stands as the motto for philosophy in modern times: the person as self is a private space.

To sum up, the historical development of the concept of the person can be regarded as a general process of *interiorization* resulting in the identification of the person with the self. Against the background of Mauss's outline of the evolution of the concept of the person, I argue in this book for a return, in a certain sense, to a general process of *exteriorization*: the person is a bodily acting being within the social order — an actor on the public stage. There are sound reasons to believe that the category of the person belongs

17

to what Strawson calls the immutable conceptual core of Western civilization: 'For there is a massive central core of human thinking which has no history — or none recorded in histories of thought; there are categories and concepts which, in their most fundamental character, change not at all.' (Strawson, 1959, p. 10) In contemporary analytical philosophy, however, the identification of person with self is not merely considered as a contingent result of a historical process of interiorization but also as a necessary outcome of the ahistorical philosophical analysis of the very problem of personal identity. To this problem I now turn.

The analytical problem of personal identity

The analytical question of personal identity should not be confused with the psychological question of personal character or with the ethical question regarding whether a person is good or evil by nature (Stevenson and Haberman, 1998). The standard debate addresses very specifically the problem of the *numerical* identity of a person *through time* (or over time). There is a relevant distinction here between two sorts of identity (Parfit, 1984, pp. 201-202; Shoemaker, 1984, pp. 72-73). My double — or my replica — and I are *qualitatively identical* or similar persons, but we are not numerically identical, we are not *one and the same* person, just as two 'Coca-Cola' cans are qualitatively but not numerically identical. We sometimes say of someone that he or she is no longer the same person as *he or she* used to be. This is not a contradiction since both senses of identity are being used. He or she, numerically the same person as before, is no longer qualitatively the same person as before. What is meant is that one and the same person now has (radically) different physical and/or mental qualities.

Qualitative change is not only reconcilable with numerical identity but also with Leibniz's *temporally indexed* 'law of the identity of indiscernibles', which numerical identity must satisfy. This temporally indexed law stipulates that if X and Y are numerically identical, then every characteristic of X at time t must be a characteristic of Y at the same moment t, and vice versa (Grayling, 1982, p. 74).[3] Although Russell the child was small and religious and Russell the adult was large and atheistic, it is still a matter of one and the same person because the elder Russell had been small and religious in his childhood, while the young Russell would become large and religious in later life. Finally, the relation of numerical identity is in a logical sense a

---

3. This temporally indexed law of Leibniz must be distinguished from the *absolute* — not temporally indexed — law of Leibniz (which is not therefore relativized by time). It is this distinction, among others, that defines the distinction, introduced below, between identity 'in the loose and popular sense' and identity 'in the strict and philosophical sense'.

relation of equivalence, that is to say a reflexive (X = X), symmetric (if X = Y then Y = X) and transitive (if X = Y and Y = Z then X = Z) relation.

The problem addressed by the standard debate — that of numerical personal identity through time — is a two-fold problem. In the first place there is the *epistemological* question: how do we know that this person today is one and the same as that person in the past or future? This question asks after the criteria for personal identity. These are the criteria that formulate the evidence we have for personal identity, thus telling us how we come to know personal identity (*ratio cognoscendi*). In the second place there is the *ontological* question: what makes this person today one and the same as that person at some other time? This is a question about the constitutive conditions for personal identity. These are the conditions that define the necessary and sufficient conditions for personal identity, thus telling us what personal identity is (*ratio essendi*). In what follows, I only discuss this second question.[4]

The epistemological criterion of *bodily identity* undoubtedly plays the main role, not only in the everyday process of identifying persons, but also in forensic and judicial identification procedures. We identify and re-identify one another in practice with the help of bodily, external features. Yet does this mean that the *nature* of personal identity consists of nothing other than bodily identity? The refusal of most analytical philosophers — and most of us — to define a person's essence in bodily terms is rooted in their — and our — awareness of the rational, moral and emotional importance of personal identity.[5]

Philosophical reflection about the phenomenon of personal identity is not limited to conceptual puzzles; it has significant consequences for all kinds of existential issues such as self-interest, responsibility and love. In these contexts, the question of personal identity plays a leading role: for example, the moral question whether this person is responsible for that crime presupposes that the question of identity — is this person one and the same as the person who committed the crime? — has been posed. The problem of the nature of personal identity is irrevocably bound up with the *importance* of personal identity.

Now bodily identity, at first sight, is not so significant and certainly not crucial in these existential contexts. Take love for instance. If the love of a person, X, would be directed to the body of a person, Y, then X does not love an individual or token-person but a person-type (token is to type as

---

4. By 'the criterion of personal identity through time' philosophers writing on this topic often confusingly mean 'the condition of personal identity through time', i.e. what this identity necessarily involves or consists in.

5. The most significant exception to this general rule is Williams (1973, pp. 1-81), who defends the view that bodily identity is a *necessary* condition for personal identity. Williams's bodily theory of personal identity is non-standard (see note 1).

individual to species), since Y's body is a repeatable instance of a specific bodily type: a 'brunette' can be replaced by any other 'brunette'. X's love would then be mere sexual desire: 'In the case of a purely sexual relationship no particular human body is required, only one of a more or less precisely demarcated kind. Where concern with the soul is wholly absent there is no interest in individual identity at all, only in identity of type.' (Quinton, 1962, p. 66) As a result, the focus of love for a token-person cannot be the physical aspect; it must be the mental aspect. Similarly, in ascribing moral responsibility and in deciding on the basis of rational self-interest, the personal identity that is presupposed would seem to refer to a psychological rather than a bodily dimension.

In order to articulate these intuitions more precisely, analytical philosophers invoke the thought experiment of 'mental transfer' (or 'change of body') (for instance, Shoemaker, 1963, pp. 22-24). If the mental content of a person X is transferred to the body of Y, then X seems to retain his essential identity. The body of Y and the original body of X appear to have no influence on what is fundamental for X: an inner personality or a *self*. Locke (1694, p. 44) already remarked:

> For should the soul of a prince, carrying with it the consciousness of the prince's past life, enter and inform the body of a cobbler, as soon as deserted by his own soul, every one sees he would be the same person with the prince, accountable only for the prince's actions: but who would say it was the same man [body]?

From this it is concluded that the essential mental aspect logically differs from the bodily aspect. The essential constituent of the person is the self, which is only accidentally linked with the body. Consequently, *numerical self-identity through time* makes the person one and the same at every moment of his life.

The analytical problem of personal identity, then, is the problem of numerical self-identity through time. What does this self-identity consist in? Both the metaphysical ego theory and the empiricist bundle theory formulate an answer to this question of the constitutive conditions for self-identity. Let me begin with the latter.

The empiricist bundle theory

The inner self cannot be known by way of the external senses; it must be perceived by the 'inner sense'. When the empiricist looks introspectively into his inner space, what appears to his mind's eye is nothing more than the *complex* of experiences, the mental bundle: 'When I turn my reflexion on *myself*, I never can perceive this *self* without some one or more perceptions; nor can I ever perceive any thing but the perceptions. 'Tis the composition of these, therefore, which forms the self.' (Hume, 1740, p. 174) In this empirical amalgam of mental states and events, however, there exists no singularity at any moment and no indivisibility through time. What, then, constitutes self-identity from an empirical point of view? Because self-identity is not an immediate introspective datum, it must be derived from mental data and their mutual relations. The unity of the mental bundle must be built up out of empirical elements with which the person has an immediate introspective acquaintance.

For these reasons, empiricists interpret the question of self-identity as a question about the *unity of the mind*. This is a two-fold problem (Perry, 1975b). Firstly, it is the problem of the *synchronic* unity of the mind (the unity of consciousness). As I type this sentence, I feel my fingers moving, I taste and smell the smoke of my cigar, I see the sunlight shining on my table and I hear a dog barking. What unifies these different simultaneous experiences into one and the same consciousness at a single moment? This is the question of the constitution of the person-phase (or person-stage). Secondly, it is the problem of the *diachronic* unity of the mind (the unity of the stream of consciousness). I have already had experiences as a child and adolescent, I am having experiences as an adult, and I will — hopefully — have experiences as a man of middle age and older. What unites these person-phases at different moments into one and the same consciousness through time? What makes them, in other words, 'co-conscious' or 'co-personal'? This is the question of the constitution of personal history.

Accordingly, the constitutive condition for a personal history presupposes the constitutive condition for a person-phase. In the empiricist tradition, this unity of consciousness is simply explained by the *reflexivity* of consciousness: 'This unity does not need a deep explanation. It is simply a fact that several experiences can be *co-conscious*, or be the objects of a single state of awareness.' (Parfit, 1984, p. 250) Various simultaneous experiences as objects of a single reflexive state of consciousness are united into one and the same person-phase. The succession of person-phases then composes personal history. To explain this unity of the stream of consciousness, empiricists seek an appropriate *unity relation* between person-phases. Such a unity relation is not a relation of identity but it is nevertheless a constitutive condition for personal history. Various person-phases are united by a single unity relation into one and the same personal history. Ultimately the question of self-identity is, from an empiricist point of view, the question of the mental bundle's unity relation. Which unity relation constitutes the history of the empirical self?

The constitutive condition for personal history, according to the empiricist, is the unity relation of *mental continuity*: 'The soul, then, can be defined empirically as a series of mental states connected by continuity of character and memory.' (Quinton, 1962, p. 59) Two person-phases are united into one and the same personal history if and only if there exists mental continuity between them. Mental continuity is serial *mental connectedness*, and this latter relation expresses the direct connection of two person-phases in terms of memory, character and talents, intentions and ambitions, beliefs and desires, and other mental features. Two person-phases, then, are mentally connected with each other when the later person-phase contains, say, a memory of a personal experience that was contained in the earlier person-phase, or when the later phase contains the same characteristics and beliefs as the earlier phase, or when the later phase carries out plans that were laid down in the earlier phase, etc.

Yet because persons are forgetful, or change character during their lives, or change their minds, or undergo other·mental changes, mental connectedness by itself is too strong as a unity relation and must be replaced with a weaker one, namely the *indirect* relation of mental continuity. The chain of mental continuity consists of a series of overlapping links of mental connectedness. Two person phases — for example X in the freshness of youth and X as old and grey — are united in one and the same personal history if and only if the later person-phase is related to the earlier person-phase by an uninterrupted chain of other person-phases which are mentally connected with one another.

The famous memory theory of personal identity, which goes back to Locke, is merely one part of the broader mental continuity theory. I deal further with the technicalities of the neo-Lockean memory theory in the *Appendix*. Mental continuity binds the entire mental bundle together and thus constitutes personal history:

> There is *psychological continuity* if and only if there are overlapping chains of strong connectedness. X today is one and the same person as Y at some past time if and only if X is psychologically continuous with Y, [and] this continuity has the right kind of cause, ... Personal identity over time just consists in the holding of [these] facts ... . (Parfit, 1984, p. 207)

The mental continuity theory of personal identity, according the empiricist, is a special case of the general *causal* theory of the identity through time

22

of continuants (Shoemaker, 1979). The unity relation which assembles the person-phases and consequently creates a personal history is a causal relation. Now on the materialist or physicalist view favoured by the empiricist, mental continuity is realized physically. So the realization of mental continuity presupposes the continuity of a physical mechanism and this underlying cause of the mental bundle is normally *the brain* (or the central nervous system). Mackie articulates this line of thought thus:

> ... I would say that it is an empirical question what makes co-consciousness possible, just as it is an empirical question what inner constitution generates the more readily observable properties of gold. And it is an empirical question, we now know at least the outline of the answer: what makes co-consciousness possible is the structure of the central nervous system and the persistence of that structure through time. (Mackie, 1976, p. 200)

But this does not necessarily mean that self-identity ultimately coincides with brain identity. Only the proponents of the identity theory of the mind (type physicalism) are compelled to the unattractive conclusion that a person is nothing other than a brain. The empiricist, however, can defend functionalism (token physicalism) in the analytical debate on the nature of mental states.

A brief digression on the mind-body problem can serve to clarify this question (Cuypers, 1995). There are two opposed materialistic theories about the nature of mental states: the *identity theory* and *functionalism*. The identity theory defines mental states reductionistically and concretely as identical to neurophysiological states in the *homo sapiens* brain. The identity theory necessarily implies materialism (type physicalism). Functionalists on the other hand define mental states non-reductionistically and abstractly as patterns of causal relations between sensory input, behavioural output and other intermediary mental states. For instance, a headache is *that* mental state which is caused by stress, fatigue and pressure on the eyes, among other things, and which, when combined with the desire for relief, leads to the swallowing of aspirins as a consequence. Functionalism does not necessarily imply materialism, but they are compatible with each other (token physicalism). Functionalists like to use the computer analogy in their theory. Just as the same programme can run in different electronic circuits, the same mental software can run in different physical hardware. Functional mental states run just as well in computers, Martians and other extraterrestrials as in the homo sapiens brain.

23

To avoid the reduction of personal identity to brain identity, empiricists can subscribe to the unity relation of *functional* mental continuity (Shoemaker, 1984, pp. 92-97). A *homo sapiens* brain is the normal but not the necessary cause of a person's mental continuity. The personal identity software can be supported by any reliable causal hardware. It makes no difference whether the mental bundle is caused by a human brain or by a computer; only the informational effect is important. The functional self is embodied in flesh or in metal, but is logically different from its fleshly or metallic form. This empiricist view of self-identity is in full agreement with the contemporary *non-reductionism* or *soft dualism* between mental (type) states and neurophysiological (type) states (Kim, 1996).

Science fiction writers are also adherents of the functionalistic empiricist bundle theory of personal identity (Dennett and Hofstadter, 1982, pp. 3-16). Following a space journey by teleportation, person Y on the planet Pluto is numerically identical with person X on Earth. However, the brain and body of person Y on Pluto are not numerically, but at most qualitatively identical with the brain and body of X on Earth. As far as their physical aspect is concerned, Y on Pluto and X on Earth are like identical twins. It is not X's hardware but his software (programme) that travels to Pluto at the speed of light. Person Y's person-phase on Pluto and person X's person-phase on Earth are united in one and the same personal history if and only if there exists functional mental continuity between them.

Conventionalism

The empiricist answer to the question of personal identity is ultimately that the unity of the empirical self is constituted by the (functional) mental continuity of the mental bundle. The empiricist view of self-identity, however, exhibits a fundamental flaw. This deficiency is a direct consequence of the nature of the mental bundle: the empirical self is a *divisible* entity. If personal identity is entirely constituted by mental continuity, then ultimately personal identity has only a gradual character. This shortcoming leads to the unpalatable consequence that personal identity is a conventional matter. I shall focus more sharply on this Achilles heel of the empiricist view.

That empiricist self-identity is *gradual* becomes apparent when we look more closely at the nature of the mental unity relation for personal history. From the empiricist point of view, personal identity is entirely constituted by the relation of mental continuity and mental continuity, in turn, consists of nothing other than serial mental connectedness. And this relation of mental connectedness is always gradual. The degree of mental connectedness between two person-phases is determined by the *number* and the *strength* of the mental relations between them: the connections of memory, character, intention, belief, desire, etc., can be more or less numerous and more or less strong. X's person-phase today is very strongly mentally connected with X's person-phase yesterday, but very weakly or not at all connected with X's person-phase ten years ago.

The direct relation of greater or lesser mental connectedness between different person-phases in a personal history is both theoretically and practically more important than the indirect relation of all-or-nothing mental continuity. X's person-phases in the past and the future which are mentally continuous but only weakly or not at all mentally connected with X's present person-phase have less or no existential impact on X's sense of identity today. Since gradual mental connectedness is the more important element in a person's existence over time, empiricists give properly speaking only a *yes-and-no* answer to the identity question. Person X today and person X in the past or in the future are partly identical and partly different:

> [The empiricist] wishes to treat personal identity as a matter of degree, and instead of saying that two persons are or are not the same person, to say rather that they are exactly the same or almost exactly the same or pretty much the same or hardly at all the same. This is indeed a very natural development of the empiricist theory of personal identity. This is after all what we say of the identity of inanimate things. (Swinburne, 1973/74, p. 242)

The nature of empiricist self-identity is related in this respect to the gradual nature of *object identity*. The unity relation for a mental bundle is analogous with the unity relation for a social, artificial or natural object — for instance a state, a club; a table, a machine; an animal, a plant. Take for example the identity of a state: 'In this respect, I cannot compare the soul more properly to any thing than to a republic or commonwealth, ...' (Hume, 1739, p. 170) Two state-phases are united in one and the same state history if and only if there exists demographic, territorial, cultural and political continuity between them. This continuity of national heritage consists of nothing other than its serial connectedness, and connectedness of national heritage is always gradual. Because state identity is ultimately entirely constituted by national connectedness, it can only be a matter of more or less. This is why the question of national identity only has a yes-and-no answer: Belgium under Albert II and Belgium under Leopold I (or the UK under Elizabeth II and the UK under Queen Victoria) are partly identical and partly different.

25

But if personal identity is analogous with object identity, then the identity of a person is only identity in a *loose and popular sense*; and if the identity of a person is not identity in the strict and philosophical sense, then personal identity is just as *conventional* as object identity, for identity is ascribed to states, houses, cars, tables and animals in spite of their gradual changes. Yet how can something that exchanges a part of itself for a foreign part remain identical with itself? As Butler already noted: 'In a loose and popular sense, then, the life, and the organization, and the plant, are justly said to be the same, notwithstanding the perpetual change of the parts. But in a strict and philosophical manner of speech, no man, no being, no mode of being, nor any thing, can be the same with that, with which it hath indeed nothing the same.' (Butler, 1736, p. 101) Identity in the strict and philosophical sense, as governed by Leibniz's *absolute* law of 'the identity of indiscernibles' (if X and Y are identical, then every characteristic of X must be a characteristic of Y and vice versa), is incompatible with any change whatsoever. For this reason, it is only in a loose and popular sense that identity is ascribed to social, artificial and natural objects. Due to laziness and the poverty of language something that *is* not the same is still *called* the same.

The ascription of object identity does not correspond with the facts, but is ruled pragmatically by convention:

> The [identity] question called for a convention; we can have it pretty much as we wish, provided we agree. And the point does not have to do entirely with language. ... The important thing here is this: the convention of the courts, or the proper authorities, will settle the matter. ..., the proper authorities may lay down a convention, a convention which is itself neither true nor false and which therefore cannot be contradicted by any actual state of affairs. (Chisholm, 1969, p. 98)

If personal identity is analogous with object identity, then personal identity is just as conventional or *fictional* as object identity. Hume anticipated this conclusion: 'The identity, which we ascribe to the mind of man, is only a fictitious one, and of a like kind with that which we ascribe to vegetables and animal bodies.' (Hume, 1739, p. 168) No identity in the strict and philosophical sense can be ascribed to the mental bundle. The empirical self continually undergoes gradual changes and replaces its own parts with foreign parts. Empirical self-identity is not subject to Leibniz's absolute law of 'the identity of indiscernibles' which characterizes identity in the strict and philosophical sense. If person X is said to be one and the same as person Y because there exists between them mental continuity, and hence serial mental connectedness, then it is only identity in the loose and popular sense that is being ascribed to them. The ascription of empiricist self-identity does not express the true state of affairs, but is based on pragmatically established conventions, just like the ascription of object identity.

The common sense view

A close investigation of the empiricist bundle theory leads to the outcome that personal identity is only identity in a loose or conventional sense. One could then draw the further conclusion that the notion of strict or real identity is merely a theoretical construct. But in actual fact it turns out that the belief in perfect identity plays a prominent role in all sorts of contexts where personal identity is clearly of some *importance*. The role of strict personal identity in existential matters such as responsibility, love and self-interest is a highly significant one. Let me give some examples.

If a war criminal is held responsible for his crimes in the past, then the prosecutor assumes him to be identical with the one who acted reprehensibly during World War II, for not just anyone — an innocent person picked out at random — should be punished for the atrocities of the Nazi Doctor Mengele. A faithful husband would feel deeply wounded if he were the victim of a so-called 'substitute bedmate' affair, for instance if his wife and her twin sister switched beds. A person does not share the conjugal bed with just anyone. If a person takes care of his own future, for instance by making pension contributions, then this presupposes identity with the person who will enjoy the fruits of his current efforts in 2025. No one takes on a heavy burden for the enjoyment of someone else.

Clearly there is a significant role for personal identity in rational, emotional and moral contexts. The common sense concept of personal identity can only play this prominent role in existential practices if personal identity is always *total*. The important identity question must always have a *yes-or-no* answer: real personal identity is an all-or-nothing matter.

Doctor Mengele does not consist partly of the Angel of Death and partly of the Good Samaritan; the person who is held responsible today is one and the same person as the war criminal in World War II. The bed companion does not consist partly of her twin sister, partly of herself; she is the wife all of a piece. The future enjoyer is not partly someone else; the pensioner in 2025 and the prudent person today are identical in the strict sense. In existential questions such as self-interest, love and responsibility, common sense personal identity is indisputably *perfect or true* identity.

As a result, in moral, emotional and rational contexts, personal identity does not play a conventional or fictional role, but an essential one. If personal identity were fictitious, then existential practices would be overturned:

> ... our ordinary view of human rights and responsibilities, indeed a whole range of our ordinary moral attitudes, is based on a conception of personal identity totally at variance with the conventionalist view. If identity is a 'fiction', then I cannot suppose that I should feel any shame for my wrongdoing, or regard myself as responsible for it. (Madell, 1981, p. 115)

If personal identity were a fiction, then Doctor Mengele could not be held responsible for the crimes he committed in the past, it would make no difference with whom one shares the conjugal bed, and no one would attach any importance to saving for a pension.

This means that the empiricist bundle theory of personal identity inevitably comes into conflict with common sense, since the identity of the mental bundle is ultimately conventional. Theoretically, this conclusion may not be so disturbing, but practically such conventionalism leads to an existential catastrophe. The empiricist declaration that personal identity is a fiction inevitably clashes with the awareness of the existential importance of personal identity. Empiricists are unable to account for the significance of personal identity in rational, emotional and moral contexts. In other words, their analysis of personal identity provides no *rational justification* for the common sense concept of the person contained in existential practices. If personal identity is only identity in a loose and popular sense, and hence fictituous identity, then responsibility, love and prudential self-interest themselves, in as much as they presuppose personal identity, come down to only existential or *practical fictions* pragmatically upheld for the sake of convenience. For this reason, 'every man of common sense' is forced to seek an explanation and validation of his 'natural sense of things' in some other view of the nature of personal identity.[6]

The metaphysical ego theory

The traditional alternative to the empiricist conception is the metaphysical view of self-identity. Metaphysicians and empiricists agree that the essential constituent of the person is not the body but the self. And just like the empiricist, the metaphysician defends the view that the self cannot be known through external senses but must be perceived by the 'inner sense'. The metaphysician's inner eye has privileged access to the deep self: 'For

6. The first expression is taken from Reid, 1785a, p. 108, the second from Butler, 1736, p. 103.

when I consider the mind, or myself in so far as I am merely a thinking thing, I am unable to distinguish any parts within myself; I understand myself to be something quite single and complete.' (Descartes, 1641, AT 68) According to the metaphysical point of view, the person's mental aspect must be understood in a deeper sense than the empirical self. The psychological dimension of the person is constituted in the first place by the *soul-substance* or the *spiritual ego*. From the metaphysical point of view, a person living on Earth consists of two parts: a material part, the body, and an immaterial part, the soul. This spiritual self is then conceived as the essential part of the person, the deep self or the 'hard diamond' which escapes the contingent vicissitudes of empirical life.

Of course, the Cartesian heritage in the metaphysical ego theory is quite apparent:

> We may say that there is a stuff of another kind, *immaterial stuff*, and that persons are made of both normal bodily matter and of this immaterial stuff but that it is the continuity of the latter which provides that continuity of stuff which is necessary for the identity of the person over time. This is in essence the way of expressing the simple theory which is adopted by those who say that a person living on Earth consists of two parts — a material part, the body; and an immaterial part, *the soul*. The soul is the essential part of a person, and it is its continuing which constitutes the continuing of the person. While on Earth, the soul is linked to a body (by the body being the vehicle of the person's knowledge of and action upon the physical world). But, it is logically possible, the soul can be separated from the body and exist in a *disembodied* state ... or linked to a new body.(Swinburne, 1984, p. 27; my italics)

A person is a self-conscious soul-substance having an introspective acquaintance with its identical continued existence through time. Self-identity through time, therefore, consists in the identity of the continued existence of the simple, immutable soul-substance. This person today is one and the same as that person in the past or the future if and only if there is *substantial identity* between them. This metaphysical view of self-identity seems to give support not only to the (religious) belief in life after death, but also to the discomforting idea that I could have been someone else. For metaphysicians it is logically possible that my soul-substance would continue to exist in separation from my decaying earthly body, just as it is possible that my soul-substance might have been incarnated in some other earthly body than that of Stefaan Cuypers, for instance in the body of Napoleon.

The initial mistake in any empiricist theory — in particular the bundle theory — lies in reducing the constitutive conditions for personal identity to epistemological criteria for personal identity. The continued existence of a person rests on *more than* the empirical continuity of the body, the brain or the (functional) mental bundle. Spatio-temporal continuity, causal continuity, as well as mental continuity, are only consumers but not producers of personal identity. The constitutive aspect of a person has essentially nothing to do with his physical and empirical mental aspects. This is why metaphysicians define personal identity tautologically in terms of substantial identity. The concept of self-identity cannot be analyzed further: the identity of a person consists of nothing less than his identity.

This non-reductionistic view of personal identity fits perfectly into the classical *dualism* between a body and a spiritual substance:

> ... only the mental side is really me, and that in so far as a body is mine it is so only because it is related to that which has subjectivity in its own right: my mind, or self. ..., if only the mental side has the property of subjectivity, only the mental side has what must go with this, an identity through time which is strict and unanalyzable. This commits us ... clearly to [Cartesian] dualism. ... I want to insist, then, that the only coherent view of the self and of its identity through time is one which recognizes the reality of subjectivity and ... I want also to insist that the only view of the mind-body relationship which can accommodate this view is [Cartesian] dualism.(Madell, 1989, pp. 39-40)[7]

The immaterial soul-substance is the place where mental life runs its course. As a result, the metaphysical solution to the problem of personal identity also provides at a single stroke a solution to the (empiricist) problem of the unity of the mind. Different simultaneous experiences are synchronically and diachronically united because one and the same soul-substance *has* all experiences. In other words, the spiritual ego is the immaterial *subject of experiences*. The ego stands in a relation of ownership with its experiences: 'Our idea of "a mind" (if by "a mind" we mean, ..., a person, or a self) is not an idea only of "particular perceptions". It is not the idea of the perception of love or hate and the perception of cold or warmth, ... It is an idea of that which loves or hates, and of that which feels cold or warm (and, of course, of much more besides).' (Chisholm, 1976, p. 39) This means that the unity of

7. See also Madell, 1981, pp. 23-26; pp. 122-140. This substance dualism is developed as well by Swinburne, 1986, pp. 145-160; pp. 174-199.

the empirical self is constituted by the identity of the metaphysical self.

In sum, as an alternative to the empiricist approach to the problem of personal identity in analytical philosophy, the metaphysical approach offers the following interrelated theses:

> ... that it [the self] is a simple indivisible substance; that it is not ontologically reducible to other sorts of entities and their relations; that its presence is all-or-nothing; that its survival can consist in nothing other than its identity over time; that its survival is not a matter of degree (since it is simple in nature); that it is a mental concept whose essence is best revealed from the first-person perspective (it is to be seen first and foremost as the reference of 'I'); that its identity over time cannot be given non-trivial criteria. (McGinn, 1982, p. 121)

Essentialism

At first sight, the metaphysical ego theory of personal identity leads to gratifying consequences not just on the theoretical level, but more importantly on the practical level. This optimism flows directly from the nature of the spiritual ego: the immaterial nature of the metaphysical self is *indivisible*.

If personal identity is constituted by substantial identity, then personal identity is always *complete*, never gradual. Personal identity is perfect identity because the person is essentially a 'monad' that cannot be split or change in a partial manner. As Reid already emphasized: 'A part of a person is a manifest absurdity. ... A person is something indivisible, and is what Leibnitz calls a *monad*. My personal identity, therefore, implies the continued existence of that indivisible thing which I call *myself*.' (Reid, 1785a, p. 109) And again: 'The identity of a person is a perfect identity: wherever it is real, it admits of no degrees; and it is impossible that a person should be in part the same, and in part different; because a person is a *monad*, and is not divisible into parts.' (Reid, 1785a, p. 111) Because of this, metaphysicians can in principle give an unambiguous *yes-or-no* answer to the question of identity: is person X today numerically identical with person Y in the past or future? This entails that metaphysical self-identity, contrary to object identity and hence also empiricist self-identity, is always ascribed *in the strict and philosophical sense*. Hence it remains faithful to Leibniz's *absolute* 'law of the identity of indiscernibles'.

If personal identity is constituted by simple and immutable substantial identity, then personal identity is an all-or-nothing matter, for if (*per impossibile*) the spiritual ego would change or split up, then it would cease to exist.

31

Consequently, the ascription of metaphysical self-identity does not need to be regulated in a pragmatic way since such an ascription corresponds to the actual state of affairs. According to this view, the deep self is not a conventional fiction but an ontological reality. This leads to the invigorating result that personal identity is always a matter of *real essence*. If person X is substantially identical with person Y, then X and Y *are* identical in the strict sense. Although there might be cases in which we have insurmountable epistemological difficulties to determine whether person X is identical with person Y, the ontological question of identity 'Is person X the same as person Y?', will always have a definitive yes-or-no answer.

The upshot is that common sense can do little else than take in marriage the metaphysical view of the nature of personal identity, since the metaphysical point of view provides a philosophical foundation for the significance of personal identity in rational, emotional and moral practices. In other words, this conception provides a *rational justification* for the common sense concept of the person which implicitly is at work in existential matters such as responsibility, love and self-interest: 'Shame, remorse, pride, and gratitude are just a few of the moral attitudes which clearly depend on a conception of persons as enduring entities, and which cannot survive the adoption of an [empiricist] ontology of person-phases.' (Madell, 1981, p. 116)

So when Simon Wiesenthal holds Doctor Mengele responsible for the acts of cruelty committed by the Angel of Death, Wiesenthal *rightly* assumes that the identity of the accused with the war criminal from World War II is a perfect identity. The grey and aged Mengele is therefore fully responsible. This ascription of the maximal responsibility and subsequent punishment is rationally justified, according to the metaphysician, because Doctor Mengele and the Angel of Death are two 'person-phases' of one and the same soul-substance which constitutes the identity of this war criminal through time in the strict and philosophical sense. It is this same substantial assurance that provides the faithful husband with the confidence that he is sharing his conjugal bed with his *genuine* wife and guarantees that the person saving for his pension is taking care of *his own* old age.

However, 'every man of common sense' will quickly come to realize that his metaphysical bond is at most a marriage of convenience (*un mariage de raison*), for the ego theory of personal identity is confronted in its own right with three insurmountable *conceptual and epistemological obstacles*.

Firstly: the positing of a soul-substance as the seat of personal identity is *regressive* (Strawson, 1966, pp. 173-175; Quinton, 1962, pp. 54-55). Metaphysicians define the person as the self-conscious spiritual ego. Yet there is nothing in the nature of self-consciousness that rules out the possibility that a person would be constituted at a certain moment by a group of egos or by a series of egos through time. A group of egos can have indistinguishable experiences just as a company of soldiers can wear a certain sort of uniform; so the experience with which you are introspectively acquainted at this instant possibly belongs to a plurality of egos. And a series of egos can have the selfsame mental bundle just as a team of relay runners can hand off one and the same baton; the stream of consciousness with which you are introspectively acquainted over time possibly connects to a multitude of egos. Nothing in self-conscious experience excludes the possibility that you are at this very second possessed by thousands of egos and, from one second to the next, receive a different soul. In other words, the synchronic individuation and the diachronic identity of the spiritual ego pose a problem.[8] Metaphysicians, in response to this problem, must appeal to the *supra-ego* in order to guarantee the unity of the spiritual ego; and, in turn, they must appeal to the *super-ego* to guarantee the unity of the supra-ego, and so on *ad infinitum*.

Secondly: soul-substances *cannot be differentiated* from one another (Williams, 1966, pp. 40-42). From the metaphysical point of view I could have been Napoleon and he could have been Stefaan Cuypers. My essential features have nothing to do with the bodily and empirical mental features of Stefaan Cuypers, and his essential features have nothing to do with the accidental features of the 'little general'. How, then, can the soul-substances of Stefaan Cuypers and Napoleon be distinguished from each other? What historical difference would exchanging our spiritual egos make? Whether I am constituted by my own soul-substance or that of Napoleon, or by none at all, seems to make no empirical difference. The appeal to ethereal soul-substances would seem only to multiply needlessly the entities in the universe.

Thirdly: empiricists claim that the soul-substance *cannot be observed* by the introspective inner eye. There is not the slightest empirical proof for belief in soul-substances: neither public observation nor private introspection reveals spiritual egos (Parfit, 1984, pp. 223-228). Harking back to Hume, this represents the classical epistemological dismissal of soul-substances in the empiricist tradition: 'Our experiences give us no reason to believe in the existence of these entities [separately existing subjects of experiences; Cartesian pure ego's].' (Parfit, 1984, p. 224)

This epistemological outcome, combined with the conceptual principle of 'no entity without identity' (Strawson, 1976), seems to lead to the disconcerting conclusion that essentialistic self-identity is a metaphysical miracle or an *ontological fiction*.

---

8. Immanuel Kant formulated this problem for the first time in the *Paralogismen* chapter of his *Kritik der Reinen Vernunft*. For a lucid commentary on this, see Kitcher, 1982, pp. 515-547.

The aporetic standard debate

If we can compare philosophical debates to the game of chess, then we could say that the standard debate on personal identity leads to a stalemate: the match between empiricists and metaphysicians in analytical philosophy ends in a draw since neither of the two views gives a satisfactory account of the *nature* as well as the *importance* of personal identity. In light of generally accepted beliefs and values — so-called 'common sense' — neither the empiricist nor the metaphysical approach provides an adequate view of *both* the ontology of personal identity *and* the relevance of personal identity in existential contexts such as responsibility, love and self-interest.

Proponents of the bundle theory adhere to the common sense idea of knowable facts and to the scientific idea of respectable entities, but they cannot rationally justify the significant concept of perfect personal identity in existential practices. Although the empiricist view corresponds on the ontological level to the mechanistic and normal, common sense worldview of contemporary Western civilization, this conventionalistic outlook undermines our ordinary existential self-image. If one accepts this conventionalism, then one takes responsibility, love and self-interest to be *practical fictions*. That is to say, if this conventionalist empiricism is received as the explanation of how personal identity is constituted, then our common practices and ordinary attitudes, which are based on a conception of personal identity totally at variance with the conventionalist view, are eliminated or at best reduced to pragmatic illusions. Clearly, the bundle theory fails on the side of 'what matters'.

Conversely, adherents of the ego theory can indeed provide a rational justification of the significant view of human nature that forms the background of existential practices, but they are far removed from the mechanistic and normal, common-sense picture of the world's make-up because of the appeal to further facts and unknowable entities. While the metaphysical view supports our ordinary existential self-awareness, on the ontological level, this essentalistic viewpoint creates a miraculous awareness of transcendent spirituality. If one accepts this essentialism, then one postulates an *ontological fiction*. That is to say, if this essentialist metaphysics is received as an explanation of how personal identity is constituted, then our personal identity becomes clouded with ontological obscurity as it vanishes into an ontological darkness beyond the reach of experience. Clearly, the ego theory fails on the side of 'what there is'.

Herein lies the *aporia* that the standard debate on personal identity in analytical philosophy runs up against: In the light of our common sense as well as scientific beliefs about the world and our ordinary practical values, neither the empiricist approach nor the metaphysical approach can ade-

34

quately account for *both* the ontology of personal identity *and* the importance of personal identity in existential contexts which involve responsibility, love, self-interest and the like. Again, the bundle theory gives rise to a destructive conventionalism, whereas the ego theory implies an obscure essentialism. 'Every man of common sense' is either stranded on the empiricist reef Scylla or sinks into the Charybdis of the metaphysical whirlpool. Are analytical philosophers forcing common sense to live under illusions? Must common sense make a choice between a practical or an ontological fiction? Until the present day, this aporia has not yet been given an adequate solution within the framework of analytical philosophy. The analytical problem of personal identity is, then, a real *problem*.

Chapter Two

Parfit's and Perry's Impersonal Solution

Introduction

From the common sense point of view, neither the empiricist bundle theory nor the metaphysical ego theory seems at first sight to provide an adequate account of both the nature and the importance of personal identity. I arrived at this bleak conclusion with regard to the standard debate at the end of the previous chapter. Now if the metaphysical approach were the sole alternative to the empiricist approach, then it would further follow that the problem of personal identity in analytical philosophy is *unsolvable*. On closer inspection though, there *is* a radical solution to the problem. In an attempt to find a way out of the dramatic situation into which the standard debate has fallen, some radical empiricists — specifically Parfit and Perry — have proposed, within the context of the bundle theory, a *reductionistic* or *impersonal* solution to the problem of personal identity.

In this chapter I want to present the core arguments of this impersonal theory. The radical empiricist – the reductionist – interprets the aporia of the standard debate about personal identity in analytical philosophy as a *dilemma*. Faced with the dilemma between conventionalism or essentialism, he chooses firmly for an empiricist conventionalism that he develops into an impersonal theory of personal identity. Metaphysical essentialism is out of fashion and has become totally implausible in (post)modern society. The reductionist sticks with his decision, and tries to live not only with its theoretical consequences, but also with its practical consequences. Although the common sense view cannot be rationally justified, our fictional belief in personal identity can be explained in terms of reductive naturalism. Responsibility, love and self-interest are not mere practical fictions, but our rational, emotional and moral practices must nevertheless be radically reconceived and revised in light of the impersonal conception of the self. Finally, I draw conclusions from the frontal clash between the reductionist revisionism of the impersonal theory of personal identity and the instinctive personalism of common sense.

Impersonal personal identity

The impersonal solution consists of an extreme radicalization of the bundle theory of personal identity. Let me present again the core of this empirical theory — discussed in greater detail in the previous chapter. The traditional, metaphysical idea that personal identity is constituted by a soul-substance is rejected as an ontological illusion. When we turn our eyes inward, we never penetrate past superficial experiences and discover a deeper self. The belief in more profound, underlying soul-substances boils down to a belief in metaphysical miracles. Persons are not egos, but bundles of experiences. The unity of the mental bundle is constituted by the stream of consciousness — by the continuous connectedness of memory, character and talents, intentions and ambitions, beliefs and desires, and other mental characteristics. In other words, personal identity consists of *mental continuity and connectedness*. Person X today is one and the same person as person Y in the past or the future if and only if there is mental continuity and connectedness between them.

If one draws the ultimate consequences of the empiricist idea that a person is a bundle of experiences, one arrives at the impersonal theory of personal identity. If a person is *essentially* a bundle of experiences, then personal identity consists *in nothing more than* mental continuity (and connectedness). Personal identity is not so much constituted by as *reduced* to mental continuity. Persons are mental bundles without qualification; persons are just series of experiences; persons are streams of consciousness and nothing more. Personal identity is absorbed completely by mental continuity; in itself, apart from mental continuity, personal identity does not exist. What common sense calls 'personal identity' is really just mental continuity.

This implies that, in a certain sense, the radical defender of the bundle theory of personal identity denies that persons exist: 'Though persons exist, we could give a *complete* description of reality without claiming that persons exist. I call this the view *that a complete description could be impersonal*.' (Parfit, 1984, p. 212) The personal description 'Persons exist' says nothing more than the impersonal description 'Series of experiences exist.' What the reductionist emphatically denies is that persons are separately existing entities, distinct from the existence of experiences. Persons do not exist, in the sense that they do not exist independently, separated from their experiences. There are no further facts apart from the facts about experiences. The reductionist radically reduces the existence of persons to the existence of experiences. *Persons are not fundamental.* Unlike experiences, persons do not belong to the make-up of reality. Persons exist impersonally: bundles of experiences exist, but separate and underlying substrates of experiences do not exist. In the latter (metaphysical) sense, persons do not exist.

This denial of the existence of persons and their identity is not incoherent or absurd. The objection 'I am not a series of experiences, but a person that *has* experiences' is interpreted by the reductionist as a mere *grammatical* fact. The belief in deeper, underlying and separate persons stems from the way in which we talk about persons. Persons — as subjects of experience — exist only in language, and not in reality. Only experiences have an actual existence; persons only exist nominally. This means that experiences do not have a personal owner; they just occur in an impersonal universe. 'Pain occurs' expresses what is really going on, whereas 'I have pain' does not. One could say 'It pains' just like one says 'It rains.'[9] In Western philosophy, the same thought can be found in the work of Lichtenberg (1983, p. 521):

> We only know the existence of our sensations, representations, and thoughts. One should say, *It thinks*, just as one says *It lightens*. To say *cogito* is already to say too much, as soon as one translates it by *I think*. To bring in, to postulate, the *ego* is a practical need.

The impersonal theory of personal identity is not particular to Western philosophy. It can also be found in ancient Eastern culture, more specifically in *Buddhism*:

> Buddha has spoken thus: 'O Brethren, actions do exist, and also their consequences, but the person that acts does not. There is no one to cast away this set of elements [actions, experiences] and no one to assume a new set of them. There exists no Individual, it is only a conventional name given to a set of elements.' (quoted by Parfit, 1984, p. 502)

The empty identity question

An important consequence of the impersonal theory is that personal identity can be *indeterminate*. According to the reductionist, sometimes, mostly in imagined cases, there is simply no answer to the question of identity. This seems to be true, for example, in the middle cases of the *spectrum* thought experiment, of which the following schema is an instance.[10]

---

9. For Parfit's denial of the subject of experiences and his impersonal analysis of experiences, see Parfit, 1984, pp. 223-226. I discuss this impersonal analysis in the *Appendix*.
10. Parfit (1984, pp. 231-243) discusses three spectra: the psychological, the physical and the combined spectrum. My version is a simplification of the last thought experiment.

```
  0 %                          50 %                         100 %
 (+)————————————————————(?)————————————————————(-)
Stefaan              Stefaan-Einsteinium            Einsteinium
```

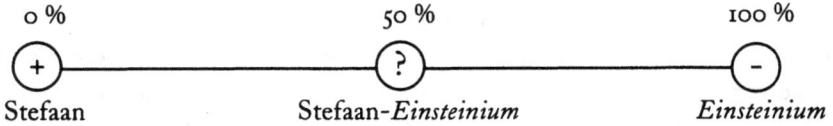

The spectrum thought experiment consists of a series of logically possible cases in which the degree of mental connectedness between — for the sake of convenience, I take myself as experimental subject — myself today and the resulting person tomorrow varies from maximal (+) to minimal (-). This spectrum could be effected by a series of biotechnological cell-transplantation operations. Tonight x % of my brain cells (and remaining body cells) are replaced by new, numerically and qualitatively different cells using the DNA blueprint of, for example, Albert Einstein as a model.

At the start of the series (1-2 %), the direct mental relations of memory, character, knowledge and so on are nearly maximal in strength and number. The resultant person would consequently be identical to me, except that he would have a profound understanding of the formula '$E = mc^2$' and would not possess some of my (bad) character traits. At the end of the series (98-99 %), the mental connection is minimal or zero. The resultant person would therefore not be identical to me, I will have disappeared and he will be a different person, namely *Einsteinium*: a copy of Einstein that knows all the secrets of the theory of relativity and displays all of Einstein's other characteristics. *Einsteinium* cannot be me, for he is a clone of Einstein and hence qualitatively identical with but, of course, numerically different from Einstein.

But what is the answer to the identity question 'Will the resulting person be identical to me?' in the middle of the series (around 50 %)? Who is the resulting person Stefaan-*Einsteinium*? Is he *Einsteinium*? Or is he me? Mental connectedness of 50 % justifies both a positive and a negative answer: I could just as well answer either way. With regard to these middle cases, it is for conceptual reasons undecidable whether it involves me or not. There is certainly no yes-or-no answer, but no yes-and-no answer either: there is simply *no answer* to the identity question. In the main borderline cases of the spectrum, personal identity is therefore conceptually indeterminate.

However, according to the reductionist, we do not have to make any important decision concerning identity here; the identity question need not have an answer. According to the advocate of the impersonal theory, in the borderline cases we are faced with a question without content or an *empty question*:

> There would then be no answer to our question. The claim
> 'This is the same [person]' would be *neither true nor false*. ...

40

> We would not be puzzled because, without answering this question, we can know everything about what happened. When this is true of some question [of identity], I call this question *empty.* (Parfit, 1984, p. 213)

There is no point to the identity question 'Will the resulting person be identical to me?' *because all the empirical facts are already known.* In the borderline cases we know exactly what is going on, because the person Stefaan-*Einsteinium* stands in a relationship of 50 % mental connectedness to me, and this is the only fact present. There is no special 'identity fact' in addition to this, above or beyond the perfectly knowable facts concerning mental continuity and connectedness. If the psychological life of the person is totally reduced to empirical mental continuity and connectedness, then we know everything there is to know about the person when we know these mental facts.

There is no further question about whether Stefaan-*Einsteinium*, or someone else called *Einsteinium*, is identical to me. The idea that this question is nonetheless meaningful presupposes that a person's life is based on the deep, metaphysical fact of a soul-substance. To expect a yes-or-no answer to the weighty question of identity assumes that personal identity is anchored in the indivisible ego, and is therefore a matter of all-or-nothing. Like the empiricist, the metaphysician does not have the required epistemic evidence to give a decisive answer to the question of identity in the spectrum borderline cases. Yet, according to the metaphysician, this still does not mean that the metaphysical truth conditions for personal identity should then be indeterminate. We do not know if Stefaan-*Einsteinium* is identical to me (*ratio cognoscendi*), but Stefaan-*Einsteinium* really *is* or *is not* — independent of our limited knowledge — identical to me (*ratio essendi*):

> When we use 'the same person' in this strict way, then, although cases may well arise in which we have no way of *deciding* whether the person x is the same as the person y, nevertheless the question 'Is x the same person as y?' will *have* an answer and that answer will be either 'Yes' or 'No'. (Chisholm, 1970a, p. 175)

From the standpoint of eternity — from a divine point of view — an epistemological mystery need not be an ontological mystery.

The unanswerable identity question may evoke a feeling of mystery, but according to the reductionist, if we remove the unjustified metaphysical assumption the spectrum borderline cases are not in the least bit puzzling.

They are no more puzzling than some borderline cases of state identity: the question whether the October Revolution of 1917 was one more event in the history of one and the same state, or whether it was a watershed between the destinies of two different states, remains conceptually undecidable. Like the national identity question 'Was Soviet Russia (USSR) identical to Czarist Russia before the Revolution?', the personal identity question 'Is Stefaan-*Einsteinium* identical to Stefaan Cuypers?' is, from the perspective of *radical empiricism*, an empty question. All answers to all meaningful questions are already known. The fact that the apparently substantial question 'Will the resulting person be identical to me?' continues to be asked only reflects ignorance of the merely empirical nature of personal identity.

The unimportant identity question

The question about the identity of a person can be an empty question. This radical empiricist thought conflicts with the common sense understanding of the importance of personal identity for *self-preservation* or *survival*. Like some moral, emotional or rational questions — the questions about responsibility, love, and self-interest discussed in the previous chapter — the existential question about survival normally presupposes the question about personal identity. In the eyes of common sense, the question 'Will I preserve my self?' or 'Will I survive?' is equivalent to the question 'Will this or that future person be identical to me?' *No survival without identity*. I can only hope to survive if the survivor of my life-threatening car accident, my brain transplant, my space journey via 'teleportation at the speed of light' or my cell replacement operation is identical to me. If this future person would be someone else, then, in the prospect of my certain death, I may as well start drawing up my will and testament. In this very fundamental matter of life or death, the identity question seems to be of crucial importance for the question of survival.

However, according to the reductionist, questions about survival and personal identity can be detached from one another, and then personal identity is *not important* anymore for survival:

> It would have ... significance whether I am about to die, or
> shall live another forty years. What is judged to be important
> here is whether, during these forty years, there will be someone
> living who will *be me*. ... On one view, this is always what is
> important. I call this the question that *personal identity is what
> matters*. This is the natural view. The rival view is that *personal
> identity is not what matters*. I claim [that] *what matters is Rela-*

tion R: psychological connectedness and/or continuity with the right kind of cause. (Parfit, 1984, p. 215)

The impersonal theory of personal identity not only has the consequence that the identity question is sometimes empty, but also that the identity question does not matter in the least. The question of identity is utterly *unimportant*. That survival should be detached from trivial personal identity on the radically empiricist view, becomes apparent when we reflect on the results of the *reduplication* thought experiment:[11]

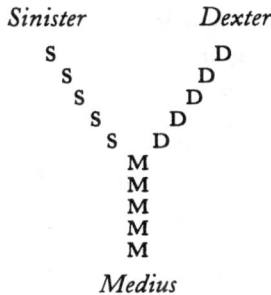

```
    Sinister          Dexter
       S                 D
        S               D
         S             D
          S         D
           S     D
             M
             M
             M
             M
             M
           Medius
```

It is not *logically* impossible that mental continuity (or connectedness) divides or takes a branching form; one mental bundle can split into two. It is conceivable that two persons tomorrow — call them *Sinister* and *Dexter* — are mentally continuous with one person today, call him *Medius*. The DNA blueprint of the dying Medius is tonight the model for the biotechnological construction of two replicas, *Sinister* and *Dexter*. Or, perhaps more realistically, the mentally symmetrical brain hemispheres of *Medius* (his left and right hemisphere are made qualitatively identical in all mental respects) are transplanted tonight in the brainless bodies of *Sinister* and *Dexter* (the left hemisphere in *Sinister*, the right one in *Dexter*). Both so-called 'offshoots' remember *Medius's* personal experiences from the inside and have *Medius's* character, intentions, beliefs, desires and his other mental characteristics. This implies that both *Sinister* and *Dexter* stand in a relation of mental continuity to *Medius*. (Moreover, the degree of mental connectedness between

---

11. Williams (1956/57, pp. 7-8.) put forward this thought experiment for the first time to reject the memory theory. Wiggins (1967, pp. 52-56) used it in support of the brain theory, and Parfit (1971, pp. 200-206) made famous and notorious use of the thought experiment in defending the mental continuity theory. For Parfit's extensive treatment of the reduplication thought experiment, see his 1984, pp. 253-266. In fact, Parfit's main motivation to study philosophy can be found here: 'I decided to study philosophy almost entirely because I was enthralled by Wiggins's imagined case [of reduplication or division].' (Parfit, 1984, p. 518)

Sinister and *Medius*, as well as that between *Dexter* and *Medius*, is 100 % or very close to the 100 % maximum).

According to the reductionist, there is *no answer* to the identity question 'Is *Sinister* or *Dexter* numerically identical to *Medius*?' after the completion of the reduplication operation. Like the classical identity question 'Is the seaworthy ship or the antiquarian ship one and the same ship as Theseus's original ship?' and the national identity question 'Was West Germany (B.R.D.) or East Germany (D.D.R.) one and the same state as pre-World War II Nazi Germany?', this question of personal identity is empty.

The metaphysician, however, will object that there is *in principle always an answer* to the identity question 'Is *Sinister* or *Dexter* numerically identical to *Medius*?' Although — like in the spectrum borderline cases discussed in the previous section — we also do not have here the necessary epistemic evidence at our disposal to answer this identity question conclusively, this does not mean that the metaphysical truth conditions for personal identity should then be indeterminate. From the standpoint of eternity, there *is* an answer:

> Suppose now we ask ourselves the questions 'Will Lefty [*Sinister*] be I?' and 'Will Righty [*Dexter*] be I?', ... then the[se] questions ... have entirely definite answers. The answers will be simply 'Yes' or 'No'. ... What I want to insist upon — *I concede that I cannot give you an argument* — is that this will be the case even if all our normal criteria for personal identity should break down. (Chisholm, 1970b, p. 188; my italics)

This epistemological mystery of fission, like that of the spectrum borderline cases, is by the same token no ontological mystery from a divine perspective. According to the metaphysician, the indivisible soul-substance of *Medius* either goes to the left (*Sinister* really is *Medius*) or it goes to the right (*Dexter* really is *Medius*), or it ceases to exist (*Medius* dies). According to the radical empiricist, however, each of the three possible answers to the identity question 'Is *Sinister* or *Dexter* numerically identical to *Medius*?' runs into an insurmountable difficulty.

First answer: both *Sinister* and *Dexter* are identical to *Medius*. By virtue of the symmetrical and transitive identity relation, *Sinister* is then also identical to *Dexter* ($S = M$ and $D = M$ / $M = D$, therefore $S = D$). But this will quickly become *unsatisfactory*. Tomorrow *Sinister* and *Dexter* could perhaps still be considered as one and the same person with two bodies and a divided mind. Yet within a week's time *Sinister* and *Dexter* will obviously be two different persons with widely divergent experiences: for example, *Sinister* could emigrate to Russia to begin a new life, while *Dexter* could emigrate to America and lead there a completely independent existence. The fact that two separate bodies are involved and that a mind is permanently divided, and its halves develop in distinct ways, makes it intolerable still to speak of one and the same person.

Second answer: either *Sinister* or *Dexter* is identical to Medius. But picking out one of them is *arbitrary*. The relation of mental continuity between *Sinister* and *Medius* is qualitatively identical with the relation of mental continuity between *Dexter* and *Medius*. There is, therefore, no reason to suppose that in the one case this relation constitutes the identity with Medius, and in the other case it does not. There simply is no differentiating characteristic that can justify picking out one of them rather than the other.

Third answer: no one is identical to *Medius*. He thus died during the operation; reduplication consequently comes down to death. But this is *implausible* for the following reason. If the mental contents of *Medius* are only transferred to the body of (for example) *Sinister*, then we should conclude that *Medius* does not die, but survives as *Sinister*. This — as demonstrated in the the previous chapter — would be the conclusion of the thought experiment of *mental transfer* (or change of body): if the mental contents of person X are transferred to the body of person Y, then the mind of X survives in the body of Y. Now reduplication is merely a *double* transfer. *Medius*'s mental bundle is transferred to both the body of *Sinister* and the body of *Dexter*. If a single transfer can extend personal life, how can a double transfer then be fatal? How can a double success be a total failure? Surely, reduplication does not boil down to death, but constitutes double, *synchronic* survival. The only difference in the case of division as compared to the case of a single mental transfer is that the extra years are to run concurrently.

The third answer is very implausible in so far as the question 'Will *Medius* survive?' presupposes the question 'Will *Sinister* and *Dexter* be numerically identical to *Medius*?' I cannot survive as a future person unless that person will be identical to me. Further reflection on the third answer reveals, however, that the question of survival must be detached from the question of identity. For although no one is identical to *Medius*, he does not die from duplication. On the contrary, duplication turns out to be a successful, double transfer. If, for example, only *Sinister* would be mentally continuous with *Medius*, then *Medius* survived as *Sinister*. As compared to the single relation of mental continuity between *Medius* and *Sinister*, nothing is lacking *qua nature* in the double relation of mental continuity between *Medius* on the one hand and *Sinister and Dexter* on the other. There is, in other words, no *essential* difference between the single transfer of mental

45

contents from *Medius* to *Sinister*, and a double transfer of mental contents from *Medius* on the one hand to *Sinister and Dexter* on the other. There is only a quantitative, not a qualitative difference between single transfer and reduplication. This difference in number is perhaps an interesting one, but it cannot imply that there are no more years to run after the reduplication operation. Consequently, if single transfer secures survival, then *a fortiori* reduplication secures survival. Like the transfer relation, the reduplication relation must be a relation of survival: from a rational point of view, reduplication *qua survival* is just as good as transfer and normal survival. Perhaps reduplication is even better than normal survival, because reduplication is a case of double, synchronic survival.[12] Therefore, since both *Sinister* and *Dexter* are mentally continuous with *Medius*, he survives as *Sinister* and *Dexter* *without being identical to either of them*. For the survival of *Medius*, his personal identity has no futher importance. *Reduplication is survival without identity.*

Correspondingly, the correct description of the middle case (50 %) of the cell replacement operation in the spectrum thought experiment *(mutatis mutandis)* is that half of me survives as the resultant person Stefaan-*Einsteinium without me being identical to him*. So in this case as well, (partial) survival does not presuppose personal identity.

Non-branching mental continuity

According to the advocate of the impersonal theory, a thorough analysis of the reduplication thought experiment leads to the conclusion that personal identity is not relevant to survival. *Nothing more than mental continuity (and connectedness)*, according to the reductionist, is important for the continued existence — the survival — of the person. That is why being divided does not amount to becoming extinct:

> You will lose your identity. But there are at least two ways of doing this. Dying is one, dividing is another. To regard these as the same is to confuse two with zero. Double survival is not the same as ordinary survival. But this does not make it death. It is further away from death than ordinary survival. (Parfit, 1984, p. 262)

The only thing that happens in the imagined case of reduplication is that

---

12. Sontag has written an interesting literary description of the advantages of double, synchronic survival in her 1979, pp. 85-97. However, Sontag neglects the questions about identity that reduplication raises.

double, synchronic survival does not correspond to the *logic* of the identity relation. As a matter of logic, identity must always be a one-one relation, whereas mental continuity can sometimes be a one-two or even a one-many relation. In all normal cases of survival — and the imagined single transfer case — the 'nominal' identity relation runs parallel to the 'real' mental continuity relation. In the imagined case of reduplication, however, mental division or branching (one-two) cannot be described in terms of the identity language (one-one).

According to the reductionist, the philosophical results of the science fiction thought experiments in the analysis of the nature of personal identity can be further extended without qualms to actual life, to how things really are or to *what is in fact the case*. From the standpoint of survival, personal identity boils down to nothing more than a trivial matter of words, not only in imagined cases, but in everyday survival cases as well. If the stream of consciousness does not actually take a branching form (*de facto* one-one), then this stream of consciousness can be described in terms of the purely formal identity language (logical one-one). Speaking in terms of personal identity is just a manner of speaking — *une façon de parler* — about the continuity of the non-branching mental bundle. *Personal identity is nothing other than non-branching mental continuity (and connectedness)*. Person X today can be *called* one and the same as person Y in the past or the future, if and only if there is non-branching mental continuity and connectedness between them (that is, if and only if there is mental continuity between them *and* there is no person Z who exists at the same time as one of them and who is also mentally continuous with the other). So, in normal cases of survival as well, personal identity in itself has no importance in the slightest. In the unimagined, real world as well, only mental continuity is important for survival. If the psychological life of the person is totally reduced to the continuity of the mental bundle, then mental continuity, and mental continuity alone, is important for the continued existence — the survival — of the person. Accordingly, from the perspective of the impersonal theory, personal identity is not a real and important matter, but a nominal and trivial one.

The fiction of personal identity

When we listen to the reductionist, we hear that the question about personal identity is sometimes empty and that personal identity is actually always unimportant. 'Every man of common sense', on the other hand — as depicted in the previous chapter — always expects a yes-or-no answer to every question of identity, and considers personal identity important at all times. As a result, the impersonal theory stands diametrically opposed to our intuitive common sense view of the nature and importance of personal identity. Since the reductionist regards his impersonal theory as *true*, he then concludes that common sense is just nonsense. The I, as normally conceived, is a fiction.

According to the reductionist, the common sense concept of personal identity — the personal I — can simply *not be rationally justified*. Yet the fact that each of us possesses an intuitive, but fictional conception of personal identity can be *causally explained* in reductive naturalistic terms. In a nutshell, (reductive) naturalism in analytical philosophy amounts to the replacement of the normative demand for a rational justification of X — knowledge, for example — by the descriptive demand for a causal explanation of X (Papineau, 1993). Such explanations systematically exclude anything that cannot be described in terms of the (natural) sciences. The naturalistic truth about persons is that, as members of the *homo sapiens* species, they are extremely complicated but nevertheless unprivileged bits of the biosphere. The impersonal theory of personal identity fits perfectly into the general framework of this naturalism. Now the reductionist programme to explain the fiction of personal identity consists in two steps:[13] firstly, a *rational* explanation of the importance of mental continuity (and connectedness), and secondly, a *causal* explanation of the importance that is still attached to personal identity (for example, in the context of rational, prudential self-interest). The first step gives a cause that is also a reason, while the second only gives a cause.

First step: mental continuity (and connectedness) is intrinsically important because this relation secures the relations of *project realization* and *identification*. The advocate of the impersonal theory can obviously not explain the relevance of the relation of mental continuity in terms of the personal identity relation: that would be circular. He therefore must appeal to other, *special* relations. Accordingly, I am not interested in a future self that will be mentally continuous with me, because that self will be identical to me. I am interested in that future self, because that self will be the best placed to realize my projects, and because I identify myself with that self.

The fact that mental continuity guarantees the maintenance and realization of personal projects is an *empirical truth* about the psychological makeup of the members of the biological species *homo sapiens*. Although the mental bundle gradually changes over time, it is a fact that radical change of the personality structure is rather exceptional. Accordingly, I expect, with a

---

13. The most outspoken defender of this programme is the radical empiricist Perry, 1976, pp. 67-90. This modern reductionism has much in common with the classical naturalistic explanation of fictional personal identity defended earlier by Hume in *A Treatise of Human Nature*, 1739.

probability approaching certainty, that a future self which will be mentally continuous with me, will have the same pro-attitudes (desires, values) and projects as me, and will try to realize these projects as I do.

There is an evolutionary explanation for the fact that mental continuity also warrants the identification relation. It is much more probable that I identify with a self that will be mentally continuous with me than with any other future self, because a self that will be mentally continuous with me is my best guarantee for *my survival in the struggle for life.* That such a self will be better placed than any other future self to secure my survival as the fittest can be explained as follows. The continuation of my mental life normally runs parallel to the possession of my body (and brain); having my mind normally — excluding mental transfer and reduplication — means having my body. My mental survival in this world depends on the survival of my body: if my body is neglected, then I die. Hence a self that will be mentally continuous with me will *normally* also have my body, and will consequently be in the best position to ensure that my body will be taken care of — fed, sheltered against the cold, and the like — and will thereby guarantee my mental survival.

Although my future self will not necessarily be identical to me, according to the reductionist there is nothing mysterious about my future-oriented self-interest. Though the relationship to my future self need not be a relationship of identity, this relationship can nevertheless be clarified completely in terms of *empirical psychology* and *evolutionary theory.* Perry summarizes:

> One wants, perhaps, a necessary truth, a transcendental argument, a reflection of the innermost structure of reality, to get to the bottom of our intimate relation to our future self; I have offered only an empirical [psychological] truth ... and an evolutionary derivation of the facts explained. ... There is nothing left to explain. (Perry, 1976, p. 78)

My interest in my future self is rationally justified, not because that self is identical to me, but because that self takes my projects seriously and is the object of my identification.

Second step: personal identity is only of *derivative*, rather than intrinsic importance. The natural fact that common sense nevertheless attributes an intrinsic value to personal identity can be causally explained in terms of *habituation* and *social reinforcement*. I will illustrate this mischievous move on the part of the reductionist by means of another reduplication thought experiment, using myself (again) as the experimental subject.

Imagine that after a car accident I am at death's door. In biochemical high-tech laboratories two replicas (just to be on the safe side) are created according to the model of Stefaan Cuypers, call them Stefaan-1 and Stefaan-2. After my bodily death, I lose my identity, but a divided self continues to exist: I survive as two different persons, Stefaan-1 and Stefaan-2, without being identical to either of them.

From a rational point of view, this reduplication is even better than my normal survival, because Stefaan-1 can pursue my philosophical projects and thereby gain promotion, while Stefaan-2 can go on safari in Africa at the same time. Although Stefaan-1 will not be identical to me, I should nevertheless be delighted about his upcoming promotion. Since Stefaan-1 will be mentally continuous with me, he will pursue my important projects, and rationally I ought to identify with him. It is not in itself important that this other person will gain promotion and I will not: the desire that *I myself* would gain promotion, and not this other person, is irrational.

The importance attached to personal identity derives from the fact that personal identity normally concurs with mental continuity that guarantees project realization and identification. 'Nominal' personal identity normally runs parallel with 'real' mental continuity; personal identity terms are in normal circumstances co-extensive with mental continuity terms. In the normal cases, the personal identity relation can — albeit in a derivative sense — guarantee the special relations of project realization and identification. But *in itself* personal identity has no intrinsic importance: 'The importance of identity is *derivative*. Apart from those other relationships [project realization and identification] it normally guarantees, it need be of no interest to us.' (Perry, 1976, p. 81) The value of personal identity derives from the value of mental continuity, which in turn derives its intrinsic value from the special relationships it guarantees. In the imagined case of my reduplication, I therefore must exclusively attach importance to that which also in the normal cases is *the ground* for the derivative importance of the personal identity relationship. In other words, I have to directly attribute an intrinsic value to each branch of the divided mental continuity relationship.

Now imagine that Stefaan-2 is savaged and devoured by a lion in the African savannah. Even though Stefaan-2 will not be identical to me, I should nevertheless be horrified as I think about his imminent fate. Since not only Stefaan-1, but also Stefaan-2 will be mentally continuous with me, I rationally ought to identify with him as well. It is not in itself important that this second, other person will die and I will not: the consolation that this other person will die, and *I myself* will not, is irrational.

However, the upshot of Stefaan-2's fatal hunting accident is that I will regain my identity. For after the death of Stefaan-2, only Stefaan-1 will be mentally continuous with me, and this non-branching mental continuity relationship can once again be described in personal identity terms: 'Stefaan-1 after the death of Stefaan-2 can be called one and the same person as Stefaan Cuypers'. But it is irrational that I should find in this new description a source of profound consolation and embrace the firm belief that *I myself* will then gain promotion. An unfortunate African event cannot give rise to a fortunate Belgian event. Personal identity terms are mere matters of form, not of significant content.

The natural fact that I still have the tendency to attribute an intrinsic value to personal identity while pondering my fission into Stefaan-1 and Stefaan-2 is the natural consequence of my *habit* of using personal identity terms instead of mental continuity terms. In contrast to talking in a fragmentary way about 'experience', 'person-phase', 'mental bundle', 'continuity' and 'gradual connectedness', monolithic talk in terms of 'I', 'person' and 'identity' is both handy and useful in social interactions. The habit of speaking in uncomplicated identity terms has a very clear and practical function in (for example) the attribution of responsibility and prudential self-interest. The simple, but in itself unimportant personal identity language is therefore *socially reinforced* at the expense of the more complicated, but intrinsically important continuity language:

> ..., identity comes by habit to be regarded as in and of itself a reason for special care and concern, ... This habit has social importance, and is reinforced: we teach prudence, and saving for old age, even among those who don't particularly like old people. (Perry, 1976, p. 88)

This is how the *fiction of the I* is stirred up and socially strengthened. Due to the social custom of using the terms 'I', 'person' and 'identity', I regard what is unimportant as important and forget that personal identity terms are only important in a derivative sense because they normally describe mental continuity relationships. A formal and conventional element of language — the personal pronoun 'I' — is thereby regarded as a material and essential feature of reality: the personal I. Yet the belief in this I is not rationally based on one or other mysterious fact. Quite the reverse, the fiction of the I has only a natural cause, and nothing more.

The I as a family of selves

According to the reductionist, our intuitive, common sense view of the nature and the importance of personal identity is false, fictional and irrational. Common sense lives in illusion. If the ordinary person — 'every man of common sense' — wants to live in the light of truth, then he ought to drop his intuitive, fictional view, and replace it with the philosophical, rational impersonal theory. Reason demands that the illusion of the I be shattered.

For that reason, the common sense concept of personal identity in the strong sense, should be replaced by the philosophical concept of personal identity in the weak sense: total personal identity, which is a matter of all-or-nothing, should give way to gradual mental connectedness, which is a matter of more-or-less. Although in real life — as opposed to certain imagined situations in thought experiments — the question of personal identity is never empty, the ordinary person must nonetheless settle for a relative yes-and-no answer. In addition, the importance that ordinary people attach to personal identity in all sorts of existential affairs — in contexts of survival, responsibility, love, prudential self-interest, fidelity and promises, pride, and so forth — must be revised in function of the mental continuity and connectedness considered important from the philosophical point of view. For even in normal circumstances, according to this view, personal identity has in itself no intrinsic value. In other words, the impersonal solution to the problem of personal identity brings in its wake a fundamental reconception and adjustment — a philosophical *revisionism* — of generally accepted beliefs and values (the common sense view) concerning personal identity.[14] I will briefly discuss the reductionist revision of the normal (metaphysical) image of the self and the normal existential attitudes, in particular the attribution of moral responsibility.

The normal, unitary image of the self must be replaced by the *pluralistic*, philosophical image of the self. This replacement must be effectuated because the psychological life of a person is in point of fact a history of successive selves or a 'family of selves.' This pluralistic view can be derived from the principles of the bundle theory of personal identity. Let me quickly spell out these principles — dealt with more extensively in the previous chapter — once again. The personal identity relation is completely constituted by, or more radically, completely reduced to the mental continuity relation. Mental continuity in its turn consists of nothing more than serial mental connectedness: the cord of mental continuity is created by a series of overlapping threads of mental connectedness. And the latter relation bears on the *direct* link between two parts of the mental bundle — two person-phases — in terms of memory, character and talents, intentions and ambitions, beliefs and desires, and other mental characteristics. The *degree* of connectedness

---

14. For a meticulous elaboration of this revision and adjustment, see Parfit, 1984, pp. 307-347.

between the two person-phases is then determined by the number and strength of the direct mental relations between them: the connections of memory, character and so forth can be few or many, and they can be stronger or weaker.

The I fragments into a mosaic of selves, because the I is ultimately reduced completely to gradual mental connectedness:

> The distinction between successive selves can be made by reference, ... to the degrees of psychological connectedness. Since this connectedness is a matter of degree, the drawing of these distinctions can be left to the choice of the speaker, and be allowed to vary from context to context. (Parfit, 1984, p. 304)

The 'I' or 'present self' is then that part of the mental bundle to which a person is strongly connected. The 'past self' and the 'future self' are parts to which he is weakly connected. Finally, the 'ancestral self' and the 'descendant self' are parts of the mental bundle to which a person is no longer or not yet connected, although these phrases still imply mental continuity.

This way of speaking about a person is analogous to talk about successive generations. The analogy, however, goes deeper than mere terminology. For just as my grandfather 'survives' as my father in a certain sense, and my father as me without us being identical to one another, my ancestral self survives as my past self, and my past self as my present self, *without* us being identical to one another. My *family of selves* does not possess a common, underlying unitary self, just as successive generations are not members of an overarching, metaphysical generation running seamlessly through the ages. Just as I am a totally different person than my grandchild, my descendant self and present self are *totally different* selves. And just as the premature death of my grandchild would make me very sad, the thought of my descendant self dying would also make me very sad. But I would not suffer any existential agony, because I — my present self — would not die; only *he*, my descendant self, would. *I* am not, as Heidegger (1927, pp. 279-311) dramatically envisages, a being-towards-death (*Sein-zum-Tode*).

Another, *impersonal* consolation for the inevitability of death is the following:

> ... future experiences may be related to my present experiences in less direct ways. There will later be some memories about my life. And there may later be thoughts that are influenced by mine, or things done as the result of my advice. My death will break the more direct relations between my present and future

experiences, but it will not break various other relations. This is all there is to the fact that there will be no one living that will be me. Now that I have seen this, my death seems to me less bad. (Parfit, 1984, p. 281)

I *literally* survive in the memory of the future generation(s).

The importance of personal identity must be revised not only in emotional contexts, but in rational and moral ones as well. This incisive revision of the normal existential attitudes is always based on the same *gradual principle of 'discount'*: '[It cannot be defensibly denied that] when some important relation holds to a *different degree*, it is not irrational to believe that it has a *different degree of importance* [even if there are some exceptions].' (Parfit, 1984, p. 314; my italics) This principle does not give a 'rate of discount' in regard to time, but it does discount for the gradual weakening of a relationship considered to be important: the weaker the relationship is, the less importance it has. If an emotionally, rationally or morally important relationship becomes weaker, then it is plausible to claim that the relationship is of lesser importance, and in the limiting case one can even say that the relationship has no importance at all.

The relation considered to be philosophically important — that of mental connectedness — holds to a lesser degree between my present and past (or future) self than that between myself today and yesterday (or tomorrow). The first relation is, therefore, less important than the second. And since the degree of mental connectedness between my present self and my ancestral (or descendant) self is minimal or zero, this relation has no importance. These differences in importance can — as I discussed in the previous section — be rationally explained in terms of project realization and identification, at least with regard to the future. For the purpose of illustration, I will apply the 'discount' principle of the impersonal theory to the practice of attributing *moral responsibility* and determining whether someone deserves *punishment*. The points I will be making also apply, *mutatis mutandis*, to existential matters such as love relationships, prudential self-interest, fidelity and promises, deserts and pride, and so forth. In this regard, the impersonal theory of personal identity generally lends support to *utilitarian* moral theory. As a consequence, 'every man of common sense' should give up his intuitive, personalist view of morality and replace it with the philosophical, impersonal utilitarian theory (Parfit, 1984, pp. 329-342).

When Simon Wiesenthal holds Doctor Mengele morally responsible for the atrocities of the Angel of Death in the concentration camp of Auschwitz, this famous Nazi hunter presupposes that there is a perfect identity between the accused and the war criminal: the old and grey Mengele is consequently *fully* responsible. According to the reductionist revisionist, this attribution of maximal responsibility is based on the mistaken assumption that Doctor Mengele and the Angel of Death are one and the same unitary self. But Doctor Mengele is one self, and the Angel of Death is quite another self, from a 'family of selves.' There is no deep, metaphysical self that lies beneath a history of successive, empirical selves as its foundation. The Angel of Death is, at the most, the past self of Doctor Mengele; Mengele is consequently only *partly* responsible for the atrocities committed by the Angel of Death. And if Doctor Mengele would suffer from permanent memory loss, and if Mengele would also have the stable character of the Good Samaritan, the reductionist revisionist would claim that he was absolutely not responsible and, correspondingly, that punishing him would be totally unjust. Were the Angel of Death to be the ancestral self of Doctor Mengele and therefore only minimally or not at all mentally connected with Mengele, then the latter would not deserve to be punished for the crimes of the former, for that would be tantamount to punishing us for the sins of our grandfathers.

Reductionism and instinctive personalism

Radical empiricists — in particular Parfit and Perry — subtly avoid the dramatic situation into which the standard debate about personal identity has become mired. But someone who thought through the reductionist idea that a person is nothing more than a series of experiences to its extreme conclusions would end up being bewildered, and even dismayed. For, on closer inspection, the impersonal solution to the analytical problem of personal identity ultimately leads to a serious distortion and even complete destruction of the personalist *descriptive metaphysics* and the personalist *moral and emotional reactive attitudes* of 'every man of common sense.'

The reductionist idea that persons exist as impersonally as raindrops is directly at odds with our intuitive, common sense conception of the nature of persons. And the revisionist idea that personal identity in existential contexts such as responsibility, love and self-interest is a mere matter of words sharply conflicts with our normal sense of value and sensibility. Of course, the fact that the impersonal theory does not square with the common sense view does not in itself constitute a philosophical argument against this theory. But our 'instinctive' and generally accepted beliefs and values seem to form the only basis upon which an adequate view of both the nature and the importance of personal identity can be philosophically constructed.

The reductionist, however, rejects the instinctive personalism of common sense as an illusion. To opt for empiricist conventionalism ultimately amounts to acknowledging the fictionalism of the common sense view. Is the ordinary person — when he sticks to his guns — then forced to live with the fiction of personal identity? To salvage instinctive personalism by revitalizing the Cartesian *ego cogito* — or another variant of this metaphysical idea — seems an overreaction. To postulate a substantial (or transcendental) I is simply to replace the practical fiction of personal identity with the ontological mystery of personal identity. Is the ordinary person at the end of the day faced with the choice between *either* the fiction *or* the mystery of personal identity?

The analytical problem of personal identity — as formulated at the end of the previous chapter — is not really resolved by the impersonal theory. On the contrary, the empiricist position in the standard debate simply becomes *more extreme and hardened*; the radical impersonal solution only adds fuel to the fire. In other words, the aporia of the standard debate is not a dilemma, but an *impasse*. There are different possible reactions to this deadlock. One reaction is to accuse analytical philosophy of boundless naïveté, to abandon it altogether and to look for inspiration in German idealism, existential phenomenology, process philosophy, French deconstructionism or psychoanalysis for another — perhaps better? — conception of personal identity. My reaction is less desperate, because I am convinced that a solution to the 'identity crisis' in analytical anthropology — or at least the inception of one — can be found *inside the framework of analytical thought itself.* The instinctive personalism of common sense need not be rejected as a myth nor exalted as a miracle. The person is not a conventional fiction nor an essentialistic illusion, but rather — as I will try to show in the following chapter — a tangible reality in the intersubjective world.

Chapter Three

Atomistic Self-Identity and Analytical Personalism

Introduction

There is something deeply wrong with the standard debate on personal identity in contemporary analytical philosophy. As set out in the two previous chapters, in view of the commonsensical (and scientific) beliefs about the world and ordinary practical values, neither the empiricist nor the metaphysical approach can adequately account for both the ontology of personal identity and its importance in existential contexts which involve responsibility, love, prudential self-interest, and the like. Again, the bundle theory gives rise to a destructive conventionalism or, in its impersonal guise, a devastating revisionism, whereas the ego theory implies an obscure essentialism. To my mind, therefore, the analytical problem of personal identity — as articulated at the end of the first chapter — still remains unresolved. If the ego theory were the sole alternative to the bundle theory, or the impersonal variant of this empiricist approach, then it would follow that the impasse against which the standard debate runs up leads to the catastrophic conclusion that the analytical framework of thought is fundamentally unable to deal with the problem of personal identity.

For that reason, I think that we cannot refuse to accept Coburn's (1985, pp. 402-403) conclusion:

> that our [standard] ways of thinking about the problem of personal identity are radically defective and that what we need is an approach that is orthogonal to the ones that have heretofore filled the literature; not more epicycles, but a conceptual analogue of the Copernican Revolution.

I firmly believe that such a conceptual 'Copernican Revolution' in the debate on personal identity is possible within the framework of analytical thought itself. Fortunately there is *another analytical alternative* to the bundle theory, or its impersonal attendant, as well as to the ego theory of personal identity.

The bits and pieces of this alternative — or at least the beginnings of such an alternative — lie scattered around in contemporary analytical anthropology. To escape from the disastrous situation into which the standard debate has fallen, one cannot but embark upon the attempt to construct an alternative solution to the problem of personal identity.

In this chapter, however, I have no ambition at all to directly solve the problem of personal identity in an alternative way. Instead, I will limit myself to a necessary preparatory task, namely the sketch of an overall view in terms of which the standard debate can be diagnosed and offered a therapy. To begin with, I describe, in the diagnostic part, both standard theories of personal identity — the bundle and ego theory — as forms of the self-same *philosophical atomism*. Thereafter, I will try to demonstrate the untenability of one important constituent of this still highly influential approach in analytical anthropology, namely the perceptual model of self-knowledge. Subsequently, I expose, in the therapeutic part, in what way Peter Strawson's *descriptive metaphysics* of the person contains the essential preliminaries for an alternative solution to the problem of personal identity. Finally, I briefly outline how such a Strawsonian non-atomistic view can be developed further into an alternative view of personal identity to which I have given the name *analytical personalism*.

Philosophical atomism and the self as a private object

Atomistic doctrines can be found not only in the philosophy of nature (for example, corpuscular theory of matter) and in moral philosophy (for example, ethical egoism), but also in the philosophy of mind. My central claim is that *both* the bundle theory *and* the ego theory of personal identity are at bottom atomistic doctrines. These two traditionally opposed theories have much more in common than their proponents on both sides realize or are willing to admit. The empiricist approach and the metaphysical approach share, in particular, the selfsame *epistemological (and semantical) presuppositions of philosophical atomism.*[15] Moreover, in a certain (structural) sense they even have the selfsame atomistic *ontological presuppositions* in common. This underlying atomistic habit of thought partially explains, I think, what is wrong with the standard debate on personal identity.

The atomistic kinship between the bundle theory and the ego theory

15. I shall not further discuss the atomistic semantical presuppositions of the bundle theory and the ego theory. In the course of my mainly epistemological exposition, I shall only take note of the parallel semantical models (and arguments against these models), without further elaboration. In any case, an exploration of atomistic semantics would lead to the very same (negative) conclusions as the exploration of atomistic epistemology in the text does, not in the least because the latter fully determines the former.

catches the eye as soon as the *middle period* in the history of the problem of personal identity — from John Locke at the end of the 17th century until Derek Parfit at the end of the 20th century — is taken into consideration. In this founding period of analytical philosophy in the beginning of this century two types of atomism can readily be distinguished: Bertrand Russell's *'logical* atomism' and John McTaggart's *'Cartesian* atomism'.[16]

On the one hand, the more recent empiricist theory of personal identity (especially Parfit's version) owes much not only to Locke's memory theory and David Hume's bundle theory, but also to Russell's logical atomism. According to Russell, an account of personal identity comes to the same thing as the logical construction of empirical self-identity. This unity of the empirical self is constituted by the unity relation R — an empirically given relation, such as, for example, memory continuity — between the experiences at different times. The relation R makes the experiences *co-personal* (Russell, 1918, p. 277).

On the other hand, the more recent dualist theory of personal identity (especially Madell's version) owes much not only to Joseph Butler's and Thomas Reid's ego theories, but also to McTaggart's Cartesian atomism. According to McTaggart, personal identity consists in metaphysical self-identity after the Cartesian fashion. This identity of the metaphysical self is constituted by the continuous existence of the indivisible soul-substance. The *spiritual self* makes the person subsist and persist through time (McTaggart, 1927, § 382).

However much logical atomism and Cartesian atomism may differ at first sight, deep down they have common roots, especially epistemological ones. Foundationalist theory of knowledge occupies the central place in the atomistic inquiry into the nature of personal identity. The search for epistemic foundations and cognitive certainty, like Descartes's method of doubt, straightforwardly gives rise to the privileged position of 'the first-person (singular)' (Russell, 1912, pp. 7-8). For, according to foundationalism, our basic beliefs are beliefs about our own present experiences. The inner space of the 'I' is the object of indubitable and direct knowledge, whereas the outer space is only the object of doubtful and indirect knowledge. The immediate, incorrigible and self-evident knowledge of the first person's mind sharply contrasts with the mediate, fallible and hypothetical knowledge of the first person's body, other minds and the rest of the external world. Thus, all knowledge is grounded in the special and privileged access of the first person to his own inner life.

Two important consequences for the atomistic investigation of personal

16. I borrow the term 'Cartesian atomism' from Zemach, 1970, p. 547. I shall allow myself to use this term and the term 'logical atomism' in a loose and broad sense.

identity follow immediately from this 'methodological solipsism'. Firstly, the atomistic problem of personal identity is the problem of *the identity of the first person*. Only the person himself can know with certainty his own identity and, therefore, make true identity statements. For no one else has direct access to the relevant facts which constitute the identity of the first person. So, atomistic personal identity is from the start considered as non-social identity: the identity of the person considered in isolation (Shoemaker, 1963, p. 165). Secondly, the atomistic problem of personal identity is the problem of (the) *self-identity* (of the first person). Nothing but the self — the mind — of the first person can be of relevance for the constitution of his identity. For his body is on a par with all other external objects in that it can only be known indirectly and, therefore, drops out as a constitutive factor of his identity. Hence, atomistic personal identity is, moreover, considered from the outset as non-bodily identity: the identity of the mind (Shoemaker, 1963, p. 39).[17]

Foundationalism tries to justify not only our non-basic beliefs about the external world, but also our basic beliefs about ourselves. This justification (explanation) of our self-knowledge has considerable impact on the atomistic theory of personal identity because philosophical theories of personal identity are in general determined by philosophical models of self-knowledge. Now, both the bundle theory (logical atomism) and the ego theory (Cartesian atomism) are grounded in the *perceptual* model of self-knowledge.[18] Knowing oneself has to be explained by something like perceiving or observing one's own mind and its contents. I briefly elaborate this fundamental epistemological presupposition of philosophical atomism in the philosophy of mind.

The cornerstone of the perceptual model of self-knowledge is the epistemological notion of *acquaintance by introspection* (Russell, 1912, pp. 26-28). This kind of knowledge by acquaintance informs the person about his own (states of) mind. Like all other kinds of knowledge by acquaintance — perception, memory and conceiving — and in contradistinction with knowledge by description, acquaintance by introspection presents the person with direct and immediate knowledge. Introspective acquaintance with the inner space is modelled upon the perceptual acquaintance with the outer space

---

17. The ontological distinction between mind and body mirrors the fundamental epistemic dichotomy between direct and indirect knowledge. At the heart of every atomistic theory of personal identity will always remain one or other form of *dualism*, but *not necessarily of the Cartesian type*. See also, note 26.
18. Note that the *semantical* 'name-object' model of self-reference (in which the meaning of the first-person pronoun and experiential terms is introduced by means of inner ostensive definition) runs parallel to this epistemological model of self-knowledge. Foundationalist theory of knowledge goes together with denotative theory of meaning.

(sense-data). Just as the outer senses deliver information about the world and its objects, the 'inner sense' — a *quasi*-perceptual capacity — delivers information about the self and its experiences.

Admittedly, there still remains an important difference between the bundle theory and the ego theory on the matter of self-knowledge. The mind's eye is much sharper and sees more in the case of Cartesian atomism than in the case of logical atomism. Although neither McTaggart nor Russell can give a satisfactory argument for the different positions they occupy, the former agrees with Descartes that '... when I consider the mind, or myself in so far as I am merely a thinking thing, ... I understand myself to be something quite single and complete' (Descartes, 1641, AT, IX, 86; compare McTaggart, 1927, §§ 382, 394), whereas the latter agrees with Hume that 'I never can catch *myself* at any time without a perception, and never can observe any thing but the perception' (Hume, 1739, p. 162; compare Russell, 1914, p. 164). The ego theorist can observe his experiences and the self who owns them, while the bundle theorist can only catch sight of his experiences. But, at bottom, both theories of personal identity are based on the selfsame epistemological model of self-knowledge: the relevant facts in which personal identity consists — be it the self or the (bundle of) experiences — are only open to the view of the inner eye.

One of the most salient consequences of the perceptual model of self-knowledge is that the self is formally construed as a *private object*. If the spiritual substance or the bundle of experiences is an object of introspective knowledge by acquaintance, then the self can be known directly and immediately to one and only one person and, consequently, must be private to each separate person. The atomistic self is firmly located behind the skin.

Two further atomistic tenets are closely associated with this privacy of the self. Firstly, the private self-portrait assumes that there exists an epistemic *asymmetry* between the knowledge of one's own mind and the knowledge of 'other minds'. Whereas one's own mind and identity is within direct reach, the minds and identities of other persons can only be reached indirectly — if at all — by setting up the hypothetical argument from analogy. The connections between the other person's bodily behaviour and his mental states are presumed to be analogous to the connections between my own mental states and my outward behaviour. Here, of course, the sceptical problems of solipsism and 'other minds' stare one in the face (Dancy, 1985, pp. 66-84). Secondly, the private self-portrait assumes that the self-ascription of experiences, for example, 'I am in pain', is *self-sufficient* and *logically prior* to any attempts at the other-ascription of experiences, for example, 'He is in pain'. Atomistic self-ascription can be justified with the aid of the aforementioned perceptual model of self-knowledge: the first person truly ascribes experiences to himself because he inwardly perceives that he has those experiences or that they occur (Shoemaker, 1963, pp. 63-64). Starting from his own case, then, the first person ascribes experiences, such as pain, to the third person on the basis of bodily signs of which he knows from his own case that they correlate with the experiences in question.

Both the bundle theory and the ego theory are built not only upon the selfsame epistemological foundations, but in a *structural* sense also upon the selfsame ontological foundations. There are many particulars — indivisible 'atoms' — separated from each other which stand to one another in external relations (Russell, 1918, pp. 178-179; 1924, pp. 333-339). This fundamental maxim in the ontology of philosophical atomism applies to the constitution of both worlds, the physical as well as the psychological. In the light of this atomistic doctrine the self is either a spiritual atom (Cartesian ego) or a collection of mental atoms (bundle of experiences). Of course, mental atoms can, while spiritual atoms cannot, aggregate into a molecular whole, but such a whole consists of nothing more than the sum of its atomistic parts. Admittedly, bundle theorists only accept the existence of mental atoms (micro-atoms), whereas ego theorists also acknowledge the existence of spiritual atoms (macro-atoms). But both kinds of atoms structurally fall under the same category of *psychological substance*, as Russell himself, surprisingly perhaps, remarks:

> ... particulars have this peculiarity, ... that each of them stands alone and is completely self-subsistent. It has that sort of self-subsistence that used to belong to substance, except that it usually persists through a very short time, so far as our experience goes. (Russell, 1918, pp. 201-202)

Because of this self-subsistent and static character, both the self and the (bundle of) experiences can exist separately from other selves and experiences. To put it in a slightly different way, either the collection of mental atoms or the spiritual atom is *objectively given* to the lonely armchair philosopher who is looking into his breast for his personal identity.

In sum, the portrait of the self which emerges from philosophical atomism pictures the self as *a non-bodily, private, and static object* with which the first person is intimately acquainted.

The dethronement of introspective self-knowledge

The single most important source of any atomistic theory of personal identity is the perceptual model of self-knowledge. If it can be shown that this model is radically inadequate and ultimately untenable, then the pivotal motivation for upholding such a theory crumbles. Of course, the denial that there is any introspective perception of the self dates back to Hume and has remained ever since a vital tenet of empiricist, and thus logical atomistic, theories of personal identity (for example, Parfit, 1984, p. 223). Without giving an argument, Hume asserted that the experiences (sensations, feelings, images and the like) are much more accessible to the inner sense than the obscure subject of the experiences.

However, beyond Hume and more comprehensive than Hume's denial, arguments for what Hume merely asserts can be given, I think, not only to underpin his denial of the self but also to support the perhaps surprising denial that there is any introspective perception of *the experiences themselves*. The first person does not inwardly perceive anything whatever: neither the self nor the experiences. Let it be clear that this is not a denial of the existence of self-knowledge as such, but only of a certain model of self-knowledge, namely the perceptual model which strongly invites one or other atomistic theory of personal identity. The upshot of the complete dethronement of introspective acquaintance with the self and its experiences is that the main road to the idea of the self as private object will be fully blocked and, consequently, that both atomistic theories of personal identity — the bundle theory and the ego theory — will to a great extent be undermined. I now marshal some of the philosophical arguments against introspection and the perceived self.[19]

According to the dualist, and thus the Cartesian atomist, the self is the *primary* object of introspection because experiences are only modifications of the self. Sensations, feelings and the like have no independent existence. Quite the contrary, they are parasitic upon the subject of experiences. Experiences are necessarily owned by the self. This principle of the *ownership* of experiences says that introspective acquaintance with, for example, a toothache automatically involves introspective acquaintance with the self which has a toothache. The self perceives itself when the self perceives (feels) a toothache (Chisholm, 1976, p. 52).

If (inner sense) introspection is thought of on the model of (outer sense) perception, then it is to be expected that the fundamental characteristics of perception are transferable to its introspective counterpart. What else could be the point of the analogy between these two modes of acquaintance? However, under painstaking scrutiny, it eventually turns out that introspec-

---

19. All these arguments presuppose an 'adverbial' analysis of experiences (sensations and the like are monadic mental events) instead of an 'act-object' analysis of experiences (sensations and the like are dyadic mental states). For a survey of these analyzes and related epistemological issues, see Dancy, 1985, pp. 143-182.

tion lacks the essential properties of perception and, consequently, that the modelling of the former on the latter is idle (Shoemaker, 1986). I briefly point out where the analogy breaks down.

Perception provides information about the properties of an object X (for example, such-and-such branches, leaves, etc.) on the basis of which X can be identified — classified, individuated and reidentified — as one and the same object O (for example, the oak tree in my garden). On the contrary, introspection does *not* equally provide information about the properties of an entity X on the basis of which X can be identified as one and the same self S, my own self. Because there is, *ex hypothesi*, for each person exactly one and the same self, we do not need to classify some entities as selves and to individuate and reidentify one among them as one and the same self. We do not need to identify ourselves: the use of the first-person pronoun 'I' is *identification free*. Moreover, perceptual identification brings with it the possibility of perceptual *mis*identification (for example, the possibility that in stormy weather I wrongly identify the lime tree in the garden of my neighbour as the oak tree in my garden). But it is absurd to speculate that, even in a hazy state of mind, I could wrongly identify my neighbour's self as my self; no such possibility of introspective misidentification of the self seems to exist. We cannot misidentify ourselves: the use of the first-person pronoun 'I' is *immune to error through misidentification*.[20]

Both disanalogies shed light upon Ludwig Wittgenstein's famous observations with regard to the use of the word 'I':

> ... there are two different cases in the use of the word 'I' (or 'my') which I might call 'the use as object' and 'the use as subject'. Examples of the first kind of use are these: 'My arm is broken', 'I have grown six inches', ... Examples of the second kind are: ..., '*I* think it will rain', '*I* have toothache'. One can point to the difference between these two categories by saying: The cases of the first category involve the recognition of a particular person, and there is in these cases the possibility of an error, ... On the other hand, there is no question of recognizing a person when I say I have toothache. To ask 'are you sure that it's *you* who have pains?' would be nonsensical.' (Wittgenstein, 1958, pp. 66-67)

20. For this notion of immunity to error through misidentification, see Shoemaker, 1968, pp. 7-8. In this article (pp. 13-15) and his aforementioned 1986 (pp. 13-14) Shoemaker additionally argues that self-knowledge solely based on introspective self-perception leads to an infinite regress and that, therefore, the perceptual model of self-knowledge is at best a superfluous hypothesis.

Consequently, introspective acquaintance with the self cannot be patterned after perceptual acquaintance with an object. The self does not present itself as a candidate for identification and, accordingly, it cannot be interpreted as a (private) *object* at all.[21]

Traditionally the epistemological doctrine of introspection has always been an explicit ingredient of the dualist ego theory. However, in spite of the empiricist's denial of the ego's inner eye, this doctrine has equally — but in a much more implicit way — been of central importance to the materialist bundle theory. According to the empiricist, and thus the logical atomist, the experiences are the *only* objects of introspection. Sensations, feelings and the like are entities in their own right. Yet this rejection of the principle of the ownership of experiences by the self does not exclude the possibility of introspective acquaintance with experiences. For, still according to the empiricist, the process of introspection can be naturalized as a brain process (involving a brain scanner) or mechanized as a computer process (involving a control module), both of which are compatible with the materialist picture of the world (Lyons, 1986, pp. 47-90). The upshot of the denial of the self, together with this mechanization of introspection is, then, a fully *impersonal* analysis of experiences and the perceiving inner eye (Parfit, 1984, p. 226; see also *Appendix*). Consequently, 'I have an experience' has to be analyzed as 'this experience occurs'; and 'I am introspectively acquainted with an experience' has, in its turn, to be analyzed as 'the occurrence of this introspective acquaintance is causally dependent on the occurrence of that experience.' (Armstrong, 1978, pp. 61-62)

But as before, the analogy between introspection and perception breaks down as soon as one tries to transfer to (inner sense) introspection both the *phenomenal* character of (outer sense) perception and the *causal* relation between the perceived object and the perception.

Firstly, sense perception characteristically involves a certain phenomenology, i.e., a certain way of appearing to the subject (McGinn, 1982, p. 8). Sense impressions are, at least partially, constituted by their qualitative content; what it is like to feel pain, for example, defines the experience as pain and makes it different from, say, sexual pleasure. However, in the case of introspection there is nothing that corresponds to this phenomenal character of perception (Shoemaker, 1986, pp. 19-20). That is because introspective acquaintance has no phenomenology of its own. The only phenomenology that introspection possibly can have comes from the introspected experi-

---

21. Note that the *semantical* denial that the first person pronoun 'I' (in its use as subject) is not a referring expression runs parallel to the epistemological denial that there is no introspective perception of the self. For this Wittgensteinean semantical denial, see, for example, Anscombe, 1975.

ences themselves. There is no such a thing as, for example, *the feeling of* the feeling of pain, with this second-order inner sense impression having its own phenomenal character. Moreover, if such a thing existed, then the absurd consequence would follow that the second-order phenomenology could in principle be radically different from the first-order phenomenology — as different, for example, as what feeling sexual pleasure (what it is like to feel sexual pleasure) is from feeling pain (what it is like to feel pain).

Secondly, the concept of perception is a causal concept (McGinn, 1982, pp. 40-41). In order to distinguish a genuine perception from a hallucination, an appeal must be made to the existence of the causal relation between the perceived object and the perception. However, in the case of introspection there is no point in transferring the necessary causal aspect of the perceptual relation (McGinn, 1982, pp. 51-52). That is because no sensible distinction can be made between a genuine introspective perception (which takes an object) and an introspective hallucination (which lacks an object) — assuming, for the sake of the argument, that there are such things as introspective experiences. It is utterly senseless to say that I introspectively hallucinate having a yellow afterimage before my mind, although I really do not have a yellow afterimage before my mind. All introspective (second-order) experiences necessarily take (first-order) experiences as objects; all introspective experiences cannot fail to be introspective *perceptions*. Thus an appeal to a causal element in the introspective relation is conceptually trivial.

Introspective acquaintance with (the bundle of) experiences cannot be modelled upon perceptual acquaintance with an object. Accordingly, the bundle of experiences cannot be construed as a (private) *object* of introspective knowledge by acquaintance. In claiming that there even is no such thing as introspective perception of the experiences themselves, Hume's denial of the self is surpassed and should be radicalized as follows: 'I never can catch myself, and never can (introspectively) observe anything whatsoever, *not even a perception*.'[22] And this, Shoemaker (1986, p. 24) observes, puts the Humean denial in an interesting new light:

> For it completely undermines the view, which motivates 'bundle', 'logical construction' and 'no subject' theories of the self, that from an empiricist standpoint the status of the self (the subject of experience) is suspect compared with that of such things as sensations, feelings, images, and the like.

22. Note that the *semantical* denial that private language (inner ostensive definition of mental terms) is possible runs parallel to the epistemological denial that there is any introspective perception of the experiences themselves. For this Wittgensteinean semantical denial, see, for example, Malcolm, 1954.

Descriptive metaphysics and the person as a public agent

My diagnosis of what is wrong with the standard debate on personal identity suggests that this debate is severely infected with philosophical atomism and its attendant epistemological foundationalism. For, if I am right in criticizing the perceptual model of self-knowledge, then it follows that the atomistic idea of the self as a private object of introspective knowledge is untenable. My criticism of this epistemological presupposition — the doctrine of introspection — makes it impossible still to interpret the problem of personal identity as the problem of the self-identity of the first person. In addition, such an epistemological criticism casts doubt on the atomistic ontological doctrine of the separateness of selves and experiences. Thus, if such an atomism is accepted, then the problem of personal identity reposes from the start on an *intellectual illusion*. Admittedly, further arguments — semantical and ontological ones — are required to show that interpreting the problem of personal identity in atomistic terms is a false start; but the initial and most important step in this 'case against atomism' has been taken.

What, then, is the therapy for what is wrong with the contemporary debate on personal identity? The vacant starting position, to my mind, should be allocated to Peter Strawson's *descriptive* metaphysics of the person (Strawson, 1959, pp. 87-116). Such a metaphysics describes the actual structure of our thought about the subject of experiences (the person) and the experiences themselves. A descriptive metaphysics has to be contrasted with both a *revisionary* and a *validatory* metaphysics:

> ... to establish the connections between the major structural features or elements of our conceptual scheme ... may well seem ... the proper, or at least the major, task of analytical philosophy. As indeed it does to me. (Whence the phrase, 'descriptive [as opposed to validatory or revisionary] metaphysics'.) (Strawson, 1985, p. 23; see also, 1959, pp. 9-11)

Instead of describing our actual conceptual scheme, a revisionary metaphysics tries to change it and produce a better conceptual structure, while a validatory one tries to give a deeper 'metaphysical' justification for what we believe on instinct. In the context of my interpretation of the standard debate on personal identity in terms of philosophical atomism, the first of these oppositional metaphysics corresponds to what I have called 'logical atomism', while the second corresponds to 'Cartesian atomism'. When applied to the concept of a person, Strawson himself labels the former theory *the "no-ownership" or "no-subject" doctrine of the self'* and the latter *'the Cartesian view'* (Strawson, 1959, pp. 94-95).

Looked upon in these terms, the bundle theory proposes a conventionalist, empiricist revision of our actual concept of personal identity, whereas the ego theory offers an essentialist, dualist validation of our common sense concept of personal identity. However, the bankruptcy of these two theories of the same *atomistic* manufacturing makes philosophically attractive a preliminary investment in a descriptive metaphysics of the person on the road to an alternative solution to the problem of personal identity. Strawson's view of the concept of a person contains, as I try to show below, the necessary scaffolding for such a non-atomistic architecture of personal identity and, consequently, suggests a way out of the impasse in which the contemporary debate seems to be stuck. In this sense, Strawson's preliminary descriptive metaphysics of the person only makes a start on the construction of a non-atomistic theory of personal identity, yet a very good one.

Now, Strawson's descriptive metaphysics of the person is founded on two *logico-ontological principles*, both of which impose constraints on our actual use of the concept of experiences (mental states and events) and the concept of that to which experiences are ascribed (the subject). I will take a brief look at these fundamental principles and indicate the background arguments upon which they rest.

The first principle states that 'identifying references to "private particulars" depend on identifying references to particulars of another type altogether, namely persons.' (Strawson, 1959, p. 41) In other words, *individual* (token) mental states — for example, this pain here and now — cannot even in principle be individuated and identified without reference to the subject of which they are states. This principle is one of the main conclusions Strawson draws from his central argument by which he establishes the ontological priority of particulars which are or possess material bodies. From the point of view of identifying reference to particulars in speech, it eventually turns out that *material bodies and bodily persons are basic particulars* (Strawson, 1959, pp. 23-30, 38-40).

How is identifying reference to particulars in a speaker's (or hearer's) situation possible? It rests ultimately on the possibility of locating the particulars spoken of in a single unified spatio-temporal system. All particulars occupy a unique position in a unitary spatio-temporal framework of four dimensions. Now, it is because only three-dimensional public objects with some endurance through time can constitute this framework that the category of material body is basic in comparison with other ontological categories, especially the categories of state, event and process. In our conceptual scheme there exists an asymmetrical identifiability-dependence of the categories of state, event and process on the category of material substance.[23] Individual states, events and processes invariably are identified as states and events *of* one or other material body or bodily person. Consequently, the identity of any particular *mental* state necessarily depends upon the identity of the bodily person which owns it (Strawson, 1959, p. 97).[24]

Strawson's first principle is, of course, a challenge to the no-ownership doctrine of the self (the bundle theory or logical atomism) (Strawson, 1959, pp. 96-97). For the proponent of this doctrine maintains that experiences have their own identities, independent and separated from whatever subject; and *this* is in principle impossible on the Strawsonian view. Token experiences are necessarily owned; they necessarily have a subject.

Although Strawson's first principle strongly resembles the Cartesian principle of the ownership of experiences, the former importantly differs from the latter as regards the *nature* of the subject. According to the proponent of the Cartesian view, the pure ego — the immaterial soul-substance — occupies the place of the subject; but *this* is also in principle impossible on the Strawsonian view. For, in order to identify experiences, it must be possible to identify the subject of experiences, and it is precisely this, the independent individuation and (re)identification of the non-bodily pure ego, which remains an insurmountable difficulty in Cartesianism (Strawson, 1966, pp. 173-75). Surely Strawson, like the Cartesian philosopher, subscribes to the principle of the ownership of experiences, but he reserves the place of the subject for the *bodily person* whose individuation and (re)identification pose no special theoretical problems in our single unified spatio-temporal system of identification.

The second fundamental principle of a descriptive metaphysics of the person states that '... it is a necessary condition of one's ascribing states of consciousness, experiences, to oneself, in the way one does, that one should also ascribe them, or be prepared to ascribe them, to others who are not oneself.' (Strawson, 1959, p. 99) In other words, *kinds* (types) of mental states — for example, pain — cannot even in principle be ascribed to oneself without the possibility of ascribing them to others. In order to make possible the self-ascription of experiences (for example, 'I am in pain'), other-

23. Apart from the *transcendental* argument, I just sketched, Strawson (1959, pp. 40-58) adduces more directly and in greater detail additional considerations to back up his thesis that the identifiability of non-basic particulars — states, events, processes, etc. — is conceptually dependent on the identifiability of material bodies which are ontologically more fundamental or more basic.
24. For a recent account of this asymmetrical identifiability-dependence that elaborates and strengthens Strawson's argument, see Lowe, 1991, pp. 98-104. An important corollary of the first principle of a descriptive metaphysics of the person is the *logical non-transferability of the ownership of experiences* (Strawson, 1959, p. 97).

ascription of experiences in just the same sense (for example, 'He is in pain') must be logically possible. Although Strawson himself does not give any independent argument for this principle,[25] it can be considered as one of the main conclusions of Ludwig Wittgenstein's anti-private language argument (Kripke, 1982, pp. 114-45).

Supposing this argument to be valid, the principle itself institutes a (semantical) *symmetry* between the case of oneself and the case of others. It rules out the possibility of solipsistic (atomistic) self-ascription of experiences, while at the same time establishing *social* self-ascription as the only viable option. The first-person use of experiental terms would not make sense without the third-person use of those terms. It follows that the privileged position of 'the first person' which is essential to philosophical atomism is hereby overthrown and, subsequently, that the primacy of 'the third person' becomes the hallmark of a descriptive metaphysics of the person. In this way, Strawson introduces a general line of thought to oppose both the Cartesian view (the ego theory or Cartesian atomism) and the 'no-subject' doctrine of the self (the bundle theory or logical atomism).

The Cartesian view is particularly unwilling to comply with Strawson's second principle (Strawson, 1959, pp. 100-01). If other-ascription of experiences is to be made to a pure ego, then *this* is in principle impossible on the Strawsonian view. For the ascription of experiences presupposes the identification of that to which they are ascribed and, as said before, precisely this, the independent individuation and (re)identification of the subject of experiences, is an insuperable difficulty in the case of a non-bodily entity. But if other-ascription of experiences is impossible, then self-ascription of experiences is, according to the second principle, equally impossible — *which is absurd.*

Logical atomism and Cartesian atomism have still another common denominator, namely, the belief that the concept of a person is *analyzable or reducible*. Both the bundle theorist and the ego theorist analyze the concept of a person in terms of the concept of a body and that of a mind (a self). On both accounts a person essentially is a mind which is only contingently linked with a *particular* body.[26] The bundle theorist reduces the concept of a mind still further to the concept of (a bundle of) experiences, whereas the ego theorist insists on the unanalyzability of the concept of a mind (a soul-substance). Thus Cartesian atomism is based on a single reduction of the

---

25. Strawson himself buttresses the second principle by additional considerations about the sameness of meaning as regards the use of experiental terms in one's own case and the case of others. In his answer to such companion questions as 'How is other-ascription of experiences in the same sense possible?' and 'How is symmetrical self-ascription of experiences possible?', Strawson clearly is steering the typically Wittgensteinian middle course between solipsism and behaviourism (Strawson, 1959, pp. 106, 108).

concept of a person and logical atomism on a double one. However, if there is some truth in the criticisms of philosophical atomism which Strawson and I have mounted, then this reductionism seems in principle to be not only impossible but also unintelligible. It seems, therefore, that the following conclusion is compelling:

> ... what we have to acknowledge, in order to begin to free our-
> selves from these difficulties, is the primitiveness of the concept
> of a person. What I mean by the concept of a person is the
> concept of a type of entity such that *both* predicates ascribing
> states of consciousness *and* predicates ascribing corporeal char-
> acteristics, a physical situation andc. are equally applicable to a
> single individual of that single type.' (Strawson, 1959, pp. 101-
> 02)

Strawson calls predicates of the first kind *P-predicates* and predicates of the second kind *M-predicates*; the former are literally applicable only to persons, while the latter are also applicable to other material particulars which are not persons (Strawson, 1959, p. 104). In the light of the two fundamental principles delineated earlier, it is clear that P-predicates ascribing sensations, thoughts and actions should apply *to the very same thing* — the person — to which M-predicates ascribing corporeal characteristics, a physical situation, etc. apply. For the (two) principles which constrain the applicability of P-predicates (experiences) require the possibility of the *identification* of that to which experiences are ascribed. This requirement implies that the subject of experiences has to be or to possess an entity, the identification of which should cause no problem within our spatio-temporal framework. As indicated before, material bodies occupy the basic positions in this framework. Therefore, if persons (subjects of experiences) are or possess entities to which M-predicates apply, then there is no problem of identification at all because their material bodies can readily be individuated and (re)identified by ordinary physical criteria. In this sense persons are quite literally *public objects* of perception: their bodies can be seen, heard and touched.

However, this does not mean that persons are identical with material

---

26. In this sense even materialistic empiricists adhere to *soft* dualism in that they require only that a bundle of experiences be supervenient upon an appropriate *kind* of body or brain (or reliable cause whatsoever) and not upon one particular body. Although a particular bundle of experiences always has to supervene on one or another particular material *substratum* of the appropriate kind, during its lifetime it can very well change from one particular *substratum* to another without losing its unity and identity, at least as long as there exists (functional) mental continuity between the different *substrata*. For this soft dualism, see, for example, Parfit, 1984, pp. 209, 282-287. See also, note 17.

bodies. For one thing, P-predicates which are applicable to persons cannot be applied to material bodies. In a descriptive metaphysics the concept of a person is *neither* reducible to the concept of a mind *nor* to the concept of a body. The concept of a person is logically prior to both that of a mind and that of a body (Strawson, 1959, p. 103).[27] The concepts of a mind and a body are secondary, non-primitive concepts which are to be analyzed in terms of the primary, primitive concept of a person. Thus a living human body always presents itself as a personal body and a conscious mind always as a personal mind. Since a person has both a bodily aspect and a mental aspect, he can appear either as a bodily person or as a 'minded' person, according to which of these aspects is emphasized. To put it somewhat differently, a person is not a compound of parts but an indivisible unity to which both P-predicates and M-predicates are equally applicable. The admission of the primitiveness of the concept of a person requires, in other words, the acceptance of a *sui generis* type of entity. Among the things that exist *there are persons*.

A reductive analysis of the concept of a person is generally thought to be clarifying and informative (X = Y), whereas the acknowledgement of the primitiveness of that concept seems to be obscure and uninstructive (X = X). What, then, makes the primitive concept of a person intelligible? How is such a concept possible at all? I concisely mention two very important ideas of Strawson which point to an answer.

Firstly, the primitive concept of a person is primarily the concept of an *agent*: 'What I am suggesting is that it is easier to understand how we can see each other, and ourselves, as persons, if we think first of the fact that we act, and act on each other, and act in accordance with a common human nature.' (Strawson, 1959, p. 112) The special ontological status of a person can best be appreciated if one pays heed to the fact that a person is not so much a passive or static being but rather an active or dynamic one. For the concept of an action equally seems to have a logically primitive character. An action — for example, writing a letter — involves *both* an intention to act *and* a bodily movement, without the action being reducible to either aspect or to a combination of both. When it is realized that the concept of action is analyzable neither in terms of the concept of (pure) intention nor in terms of the concept of bodily movement, it becomes intelligible why the concept of the centre of agency — the person — should be unanalyzable as well.

Secondly, the primitive concept of a person is first and foremost the concept of an object of *reactive attitudes and feelings*: '... we should think, ..., of

27. For Strawson's own statement of the logical derivativeness of the concept of a body, see Strawson, 1980, pp. 272-273.

the kind of importance we attach to the attitudes and intentions towards us of those who stand in these relationships to us, and of the kinds of *reactive* attitudes and feelings to which we ourselves are prone.' (Strawson, 1962, p. 6)[28] We not only act, and act on each other, but also react to each other in accordance with a common human nature. Now, these moral and emotional reactions are primitive in the sense of not being founded on a belief about the (inner) constitution of persons. We do not morally and emotionally react to other people because they have bodies of a certain kind or because they have minds of a certain type; we simply and immediately react to other people as other persons. So the primitiveness of the concept of the object of these reactions — the person — corresponds with the primitiveness of the reactive attitudes and feelings themselves. In other words, it is because people *quasi*-instinctively react to one another as persons that the primitive concept of a person is possible at all.

In sum, the portrait of the person which emerges from Strawson's descriptive metaphysics pictures the person as *a bodily, public, and dynamic agent* who engages with other persons and the world.

Towards analytical personalism

Starting from the building blocks made available by Strawson's descriptive metaphysics of the person, it is possible, I think, to construct a more satisfactory theory of both the nature and the importance of personal identity. For, if a person initially is defined as a bodily, public and dynamic agent, then we do not have to go beyond the facts as we know them to account for the significant role which the person plays in our ordinary rational, moral and emotional practices. When this portrait of the person replaces that of the atomistic self, the *moral agent* enters on the scene as a *commonsensical reality*. Let me elaborate on this fundamental Strawsonian insight.

Strawson's non-atomistic view conceptually describes the place of persons as moral agents in our commonsensical scheme of reality. Such a descriptive metaphysics stays in line with our 'instinctive' and generally accepted beliefs and values. In view of the fact that a Strawsonian view acknowledges the primitiveness of the concept of a person — persons as basic particulars have a *sui generis* existence — it is neither revisionary nor validatory. That is to say, such a view is neither conventionalist in the manner of the empiricist bundle theory nor essentialist in the same way as the dualist ego theory. As a consequence, Strawson's non-atomistic view of the person is in full harmony

---

28. Strawson's idea of reactive attitudes and feelings is very similar to Wittgenstein's idea of *an attitude towards a soul*. For an exciting exploration of these two closely related ideas, see Cockburn, 1990, pp. 3-52.

with the instinctive personalism of common sense: *every man of common sense* cannot but subscribe to Strawson's personalist descriptive metaphysics and his personalist moral and emotional reactive attitudes. So, given the Strawsonian view, the instinctive personalism of common sense need not be discarded as a myth nor exalted as a miracle. As a result, a Strawsonian view of the person is, I submit, the only viable basis upon which an adequate view of both the *nature* and the *importance* of personal identity can be philosophically constructed. Since the person as a moral agent is a tangible reality in the intersubjective world of common sense and science, one does not have to postulate a substantial (or transcendental) I in order to account for the importance of personalism in rational, emotional and moral contexts. Because the person as a commensensical reality is the subject of (moral) reactive attitudes and feelings, a Strawsonian view can provide a rational justification for the common sense concept of the person contained in existential practices which involve responsibility, love, prudential self-interest, and the like. So, given the Strawsonian view, the ordinary person is not faced with the choice between either a practical fiction or an ontological mystery. In sum, Strawson's view of the person promisingly points towards an escape route out of the impasse into which the standard debate on personal identity has become stuck.

I have reached this promising consequence and the conclusion stated above — that the person is a bodily, public and dynamic agent who engages with other persons and the world — *within the bounds of analytical philosophy.* To carry out my diagnosis of, and to suggest a therapy for what is wrong with the standard debate on personal identity, I have not invoked any other philosophical tradition, such as German idealism, process philosophy, existential phenomenology or postmodern deconstructionism. Rather, my refutation of philosophical atomism and my subsequent employment of descriptive metaphysics have taken place within the framework of mainstream 20th-century English-language philosophy. In conclusion, I sketch the way in which a non-atomistic theory of personal identity could be developed out of Strawson's preliminary descriptive metaphysics of the person. Since such a theory builds upon a personalist metaphysics which honours the instinctive personalism of common sense within an analytical framework, I call this position *analytical personalism*.[29] Strawson's descriptive metaphysics is an excellent tool to melt down the two erroneous positions in the standard debate on personal identity and, subsequently, to forge the scaffolding of a 'Copernican Revolution' in that debate. Although I have no ambition to completely solve the problem of personal identity in this book, analytical personalism constitutes, to my mind, a serious analytical alternative to the bundle theory, or its impersonal attendant, as well as to the ego

theory of personal identity. According to analytical personalism, the phenomenon of personal identity is complex and multi-layered as it comprises
bodily identity, *agential* identity and *narrative* identity. Unlike the bundle
theory and ego theory, my alternative view is thus a hybrid view of personal
identity. My only limited goal here is to delineate the beginnings of such an
alternative in order to escape from the disastrous situation into which the
standard debate has fallen. I will briefly highlight the essential features of
this alternative view.

According to Strawson's descriptive metaphysics, the concept of a person
is neither reducible to that of a mind nor to that of a body. Furthermore, this
primitive concept of a person is that of a dynamic agent related to the public
world. In addition, it is the concept of an object of (moral) reactive attitudes
and feelings. Hence, on a Strawsonian view, a person is a moral agent who
has a body and a mind. Setting aside the aspect of moral agency for the
moment, saying that the primitive concept of a person is that of an indivisible unity to which both P-predicates and M-predicates are equally applicable is the same as saying that such a concept conceives of a person as a
substantial *psychophysical unity*. Accordingly, personal identity consists in the
identity of a substantial psychophysical unity. Now the best interpretation of
this psychophysical personalism in contemporary analytical anthropology
has, in my opinion, been given by David Wiggins (1980; 1987). Wiggins's
interpretation is *neo-Aristotelian* in the sense that it conceives of a person as
a living human organism with the powers of intellect, will and memory —
or, for short, as a *rational animal*:

> ... a persisting material entity essentially endowed with the bio-
> logical potentiality for the exercise of *all* the faculties and
> capacities conceptually constitutive of personhood — sen-
> tience, desire, belief, motion, memory, and the various other
> elements which are involved in the particular mode of *activity*

---

29. Although analytical personalism has no direct connection with the *Catholic personalism*
of, for example, Emmanuel Mounier (1950), it is possible to develop analytical personalism in the direction of a Catholic Aristotelian-Thomistic view of personal identity; for
this exercise in 'analytical Thomism', see my 1998a, pp. 363-368. In addition, it is worthwhile pointing out a parallel between analytical and *continental personalism*. Surprisingly
perhaps, Strawson's analytical picture mirrors an important picture of the person in the
continental tradition of philosophizing. Max Scheler's phenomenology of the person also
acknowledges the primitiveness of the concept of a person: 'The use of the word *person* in
language already reveals that the form of unity meant by this term has nothing to do with
the form of unity of the "consiousness"-object of inner perception or consequently the
"ego" (either the "ego" in opposition to a "thou" or the "ego" in opposition to the "outer
world"). For *person*, unlike these terms, is an absolute, not a feelably *relative* name. ...
What we mean by the term *person*, in contrast to the ego, is something of a self-sufficient
totality.' (Scheler, 1913-1916, pp. 389-390) To conceive of the person as 'a self-sufficient
totality' amounts to the same thing as recognizing the irreducible nature of the person.

that marks the extension of the concept of person. (Wiggins, 1980, p. 160)

Correspondingly, personal identity consists in the identity of a rational animal. Let me spell out a bit this first essential ingredient of analytical personalism.

An essential component of personal identity is animal identity which, of course, comprises *bodily identity*. Because a person is a psychophysical unity (and a basic particular), personal identity necessarily involves 'incarnational' identity. The view that bodily identity is always a necessary condition of personal identity goes back to Bernard Williams's non-standard corporeal theory of personal identity (Williams, 1973, pp. 1-81). On this view, person X today is one and the same person as person Y at some past or future time *only if* X is bodily continuous with Y; that is to say, only if X's whole body is causally continuous with Y's whole body in the unitary spatio-temporal framework. However, what is needed to analyze this incarnational identity is not the atomistic concept of *res extensa* but the *non-Cartesian, Aristotelian* concept of a living human organism, as revitalized by Wiggins. Correspondingly, the essential bodily aspect of personal identity does not so much depend upon the identity of 'a lump or other quantity of matter' but rather on the spatio-temporal (and causal) continuity of a *personal* body:

> A person is material in the sense of being essentially consti-
> tuted [realized, composed] by matter; but in some strict and
> different sense of 'material', viz. being definable or properly
> describable in terms of the concepts of the sciences of matter
> (physics, chemistry, and biology even) *person* is not a material
> concept. ... For the continuity principle defines a material
> entity in the 'matter-constituted' ['matter-realized', 'matter-
> composed'] sense of 'material', while leaving it possible for the
> concept of *person* to be primitive relative to the concepts that
> pull their weight in the sciences of matter and primitive relative
> to the concept *human body*. If we understand what a living per-
> son or an animal is, then we may define the body of one as that
> which realizes or constitutes it while it is alive and will be left
> over when, succumbing to entropy, it dies. (Wiggins, 1980, p.
> 164)

Analytical, psychophysical personalism emphatically is *not mere animalism*. On the latter view, I just *am* (identical with) my body; I am just a living human organism, which began to exist as a single cell (a zygote) and which will go on existing until its biological death (Snowdon, 1990; Thomson, 1998; Olson, 1997). The ontological necessary *and sufficient* condition for personal identity is simply that of a living human organism: person X today is one and the same person as person Y at some past or future time *if and only if* X's whole body is identical with Y's whole body; that is, if and only if X is bodily continuous with Y. The difference between analytical personalism and mere animalism can be explained by making use of the distinction between the 'is' of *identity* and the 'is' of *constitution* (realization, composition). The explanation draws on an analogy with the relation between a statue — for example, Rodin's *The Thinker* — and the lump of bronze which constitutes it. The relation between a person and his body is like that between The Thinker and the lump of bronze of which it is composed. Because there are changes which The Thinker can survive but which the lump of bronze cannot (for example, losing its left hand), and vice versa (for example, being melted and solidified again as one of *The Citizens of Calais*), the statue and the lump of bronze are *distinct* objects — that is, are not identical with one another — although they are *not separate* objects, as would be The Thinker and one of The Citizens of Calais. Statues are not identical with lumps of bronze, even though they are constituted by them. Likewise, persons are not identical with their bodies, even though they are composed by them. So in claiming that a person *is* his body, mere animalism uses the 'is' of identity, whereas analytical personalism uses the 'is' of constitution. By using this constitutive 'is' analytical personalism creates the necessary conceptual space to hold that persons *transcend* their bodies.

Although bodily identity essentially composes personal identity, the latter is not reducible to the former. Like Rodin's The Thinker is constituted by a particular lump of bronze without being identical to it, a person is constituted by a particular living human organism without being identical to it. In other words, bodily identity is a necessary but *not a sufficient condition* of personal identity. Since identity of body is not a sufficient condition of personal identity, according to analytical personalism, other considerations, of *personal* characteristics, must be invoked. Wherein then does personal identity consist *over and above* bodily identity? To answer this question, the the second essential ingredient of analytical personalism must come into play. The conceptual development of this element starts from the Strawsonian thought that the concept of a person, as primitive relative to that of a body, is the concept of a dynamic agent related to the public world. As constituted by a living human organism, a person exhibits a particular mode of activity that marks him off as an agent. In comparison with other animals, the rational animal lives in a specific active mode, namely the mode of *intentional agency*. Correspondingly, personal identity necessarily comprises *agen-*

tial identity besides bodily identity. So both the 'minimal' structure of bodily identity and the 'maximal' structure of agential identity determine the *nature* of personal identity. Moreover, the *importance* of personal identity also stems from this identity of the person as an agent. Before expanding on the significance of personal identity in terms of narrativity, let me comment a bit on the second core feature of analytical personalism.

The best account of intentional agency in contemporary analytical anthropology has, to my mind, been given by Donald Davidson (1980). According to his causal theory of action, a bodily movement is an action if and only if the movement is appropriately caused by beliefs and desires (P-predicates with propositional content or propositional attitudes). More specifically, Davidson (1980, p. 87) defines acting with an intention as acting for a reason: '... an action is performed with a certain intention if it is caused in the right way by attitudes and beliefs that rationalize it.' The beliefs and other propositional attitudes constitute the reason why the action was performed. Now Davidson's causal theory of action in psychology forms a part of his wider theory of rational (and radical) interpretation in semantics (Davidson, 1984). In view of that, actions are rationally interpreted in terms of propositional attitudes from the 'third person' standpoint — a standpoint which is also the hallmark of Strawson's descriptive metaphysics of the person. In light of the rationalization principle, those attitudes should be ascribed to the agent as to provide good reasons for his actions.

The relation between the nature of intentional agency and agential identity becomes apparent when one important tenet of Davidson's interpretation theory is put to the fore, namely the *holism* of the mental. What does the holistic character of propositional attitudes and intentional action involve? Attitudes and actions cannot be identified atomistically, i.e. on their own, isolated and cut off from other attitudes and actions. In order to demarcate what they are, attitudes and actions have to be related to other attitudes and actions. Rational relations amongst attitudes and actions make them what they are. Such relations are *constitutive* of the propositional attitudes and intentional actions. So the attitudes and actions form a logically coherent whole or network. Davidson (1982, pp. 320-321) makes this holism of the mental clear as follows:

> We identify thoughts [beliefs and other propositional attitudes], distinguish between them, describe them for what they are, only as they can be located within a dense network of beliefs. ... To have a single propositional attitude is to have a largely correct logic, in the sense of having a pattern of beliefs that logically cohere. ... The point extends to intentional

78

action. Intentional action is action that can be explained in terms of beliefs and desires whose propositional content rationalize the action.

Now the important thing about the holism of the mental with regard to personal identity is that in virtue of this holism the attitudes and actions are unified in rational patterns at a time and also over time. If I form the intention to do something in the (near) future, then my intention is only rationally intelligible if it is a part of a diachronic network of other intentions, beliefs, desires and other propositional attitudes. In executing my plan of action all the different actions performed to reach my goal only make sense if they belong to a diachronic sequence of actions that logically cohere. Attitudes and actions are thus intrinsically unified in virtue of the holistic rationalization principle. Such patterns of unified propositional attitudes and, in particular, sequences of unified intentional actions are *constitutive* of agential identity. So agential identity through time is just the playing out over time of the holistic nature of the attitudes and actions.

According to analytical personalism, agential identity must be grafted on bodily identity for the full determination of *personal* identity. Some will object, however, that this additional maximal structure of agential identity cannot possibly capture our *internal sense of identity*. In reply, let me adumbrate how analytical personalism handles the internal aspects of personal identity. Of course, the capacity for agency depends upon the powers of intellect, will and memory. And these powers of the mind are in the case of persons *self-consciously* exercised. The self-conscious or reflexive employment of intellect, will and memory in the production of actions is then responsible for the *subjective* sense of agential identity and, moreover, the person's *ownership* of a particular body. That is to say, the involvement of reflexivity in agential and bodily identity constitutes the fact that *I* produce these bodily movements and the fact that this moving body is *my* body (Madell, 1976; Ayer, 1963). So whereas bodily identity determines personal identity from 'the outside' or third-person perspective, agential identity determines it from 'the inside' or first-person perspective. What is more, from this first-person perspective — in self-consciousness and memory — a person is continuously and immediately present to himself. This immediate and continuous *self-presence* makes self-identification superfluous. However, although a person does not have to identify or reidentify himself from the inside, self-presence in self-consciousness and memory is intelligible only as a subjective angle on something that has more to it than the subjective angle reveals, namely the career of an objective continuant — a personal body — in the unitary spatio-temporal framework (McDowell, 1997).[30]

Agential identity (together, of course, with basic bodily identity) not only determines the nature of personal identity, it also establishes its *importance*. In a way, however, agential identity is too 'thin' to accomplish this; a more 'thick' maximal structure of personal identity is needed to account for its importance. As the third, and last, crucial feature of analytical personalism I, therefore, bring in *narrative* identity. Yet thick narrative identity is in a way not a separate maximal structure on top of thin agential identity. Narrative and agential identity belong to the same level. Narrative identity is just the more existential and more literary corollary of agential identity. Narrative identity only introduces additional and richer methods for the unification of a person's life. According to the narrativity theory of personal identity, actions and other events in a person's life are unified into a single life by means of a coherent and intelligible life story or biographical narrative. Alisdair MacIntyre (1985, p. 218) is a well-known proponent of this theory:

> It does follow ... that all attempts to elucidate the notion of personal identity independently of and in isolation from the notions of narrative, intelligibility and accountability are bound to fail. ... In what does the unity of an individual life consist? The answer is that its unity is the unity of a narrative embodied in a single life.[31]

Narrativity internally unifies the different actions of a person into a single coherent story and it externally relates them to the wider community in which he lives. Telling the story of one's life involves rendering one's deeds and omissions intelligible not only to oneself but also to others with whom one entertains multifarious relations in a public common world. Furthermore, besides just telling one's life story, one also takes responsibility for it. Now taking responsibility for one's life story involves acknowledging its *importance*. It is then in this way that one's biographical narration plays an important role in rational, moral and emotional practices. So the concept of personal identity contained in existential practices which comprise responsi-

---

30. For interesting recent developments — which are compatible with analytical personalism — of how the subjective (self-conscious) and the objective (bodily) standpoints can combine in the constitution of personal identity and self-knowledge, see Campbell, 1994 and Cassam, 1997.
31. For a recent detailed version of the narrativity theory, see Schechtman, 1996. The idea of narrative identity is, of course, also prominent in continental philosophy: see, for example, Ricoeur, 1990.

bility, love, prudential self-interest, and the like is the concept of narrative identity. One's biographical narration is the proper object of the (moral) reactive attitudes and feeling of one's own and other people. These reactions testify to the significance with which persons invest their life stories. In this manner narrativity gives substance to the Strawsonian thought that the concept of a person is the concept of an object of (moral) reactive attitudes and feelings. Hence the importance of personal identity stems from the identity of the person as a rational and moral agent telling his life story. In sum, according to analytical personalism, personal identity as agential, and by implication, bodily identity essentially consists in the narrative unity of the actions of a rational and moral agent in a social setting and within a historical tradition.

My final thought in the first part of this book concerns the problem of *the self.* This problem should not be confused with that of personal identity. The self is a secondary, derivative concept which has to be understood in terms of the primary, primitive concept of the person. Of course, I do not object to the use of the term 'self' when it just means the self-conscious (bodily) person. Unfortunately, the term is mostly used to refer to the atomistic (private) self: the Cartesian ego or the Humean bundle of experiences. If there is some truth in my criticisms of philosophical atomism, then this atomistic use is highly objectionable. So, to avoid possible confusion, I suggest we drop the term 'self' altogether in the debate on personal identity and exclusively reserve it for the debate on *free action* and *free will.* The self only makes an appearance, I hypothesize, in the context of personal autonomy, weakness of the will and self-deception. There is no need to introduce the concept of the self, except in special cases where the person is either in trouble (weakness of the will, self-deception) or at his best (personal autonomy). I will explore the connection between the self and personal autonomy in the next part of the book.

Admittedly, my sketchy remarks stand in need of much more elaboration and they do not conclusively show that a non-atomistic view in accord with Strawsonian principles is in the last analysis a fruitful and stable position to take in the debate on the nature and importance of personal identity. But whatever the final details of such an alternative view — analytical personalism — may be, something along these lines *must* be true, unless we are willing to acquiesce in the dualistic dissolution of our psychophysical unified nature or, even worse, in the empiricist elimination of the significant role of our identity in common practices.

PART II
PERSONAL AUTONOMY

Chapter Four

Hierarchical Autonomy, Self-Identification and Self-Evaluation

Introduction

Those opposed to a view of the person and his identity from the third-person perspective, as defended by me in the last chapter of the first part, object that such a non-atomistic view throws away the baby with the bath water. They complain that if the person is nothing but a bodily, public and dynamic agent with a bodily, agential and narrative identity, then there is no place left anymore for the inner personality or *self* of the person.

Proponents of a non-atomistic picture of the person and his identity can, however, reply that even on the primacy of the third person the concept of the self need not be discarded, although this concept still remains derived from the primitive concept of the person. Only the primitive concept of the self as a non-bodily, private and static object is rejected in the light of Strawson's descriptive metaphysics of the person. Moreover, the reply continues, the concept of the self is not so much an epistemological-ontological concept as it is a moral-existential one. My general suggestion to solve the problem of the self is then that the concept of the self has to be located in the more existential contexts of weakness of will (*akrasia*), self-deception and personal autonomy. The self has to do with the most problematic aspects of action. The solution to the problem of the self is, somewhat enigmatically formulated, that the self is a problem:

> A long time ago I participated in an evening of philosophical discussion in the home of a colleague. ... I was sure that my colleague did not mean merely that the self *posed* a problem. He meant that the self *was* a problem — that its nature was *to be* a problem. (Johnstone, Jr., 1970, p. xi)

I put aside the relation between the self and 'rational pathologies' — contradictions of the mind, such as weakness of will and self-deception (Elster, 1984, pp. 172-179). In this book I exclusively limit myself to a further elaboration of the connection between the constitution of the self and personal autonomy. In this chapter, following a clarification of the concept of the self, I shall critically reflect on the concept of personal autonomy as analyzed in the so-called 'hierarchical' model, in order to propose some amendments to the notions of self-identification and self-evaluation which are of the utmost importance to this model. The main result of my proposal will be the substitution of the concept of extreme personal autonomy by that of caring about oneself — that is to say, the replacement of an extremely autonomous view by a moderately heteronomous view of personal autonomy.

The self as a higher-order intentional system

Although most philosophers use the term (and the concept) 'person' as a synonym for the term 'self', it is advisable not to lose sight of the difference in meaning between the two. In a moral and existential context, the term 'person' refers to our membership in the moral community of persons (Tooley, 1986), whereas the term 'self' refers more to our *existential essence*, or the most significant and problematic aspect of our lives. In an epistemological and ontological context, the term 'person' refers to the bodily, public and dynamic subject, while the term 'self' refers more to the *reflexive structure of the mind* or the person's mental reflexivity. As an incidental remark, I should point out that in normal usage, the term 'self' — the prefix or suffix 'self' as in 'self-protection' and 'he himself' — usually does not function as a noun referring to a concrete entity, but rather as a demonstrative pronoun expressing a reflexive relation. As a result, in philosophy and the humanities, the term 'self' is inevitably used in a more or less technical sense. Once this terminological question has been cleared up and the respective meanings have been clarified, I have no objection to the terms 'person' and 'self' being used interchangeably. In the second part of this book I shall only use these terms as they refer to the reflexive structure of the person's mind and his existential essence.

From the point of view of Strawson's descriptive metaphysics of the person, the concept of the self must be derived from the primitive concept of the person. In light of the methodological primacy of the third person, the crucial link in this conceptual derivation is the concept of *action*:

> Among the things that we observe, ..., are the movements of bodies similar to [our own] ... It is important that we should understand such movements, for they bear on and condition our own; and in fact we understand them, we interpret them, ... But this is to say that we see such movements as *actions*, that we interpret them in terms of intention, ... (Strawson, 1959, pp. 111-112)

86

The primitive concept of a person is in the first place the concept of an acting being or an agent. Although Strawson does not further elaborate this point, the conceptual link between action and the self can to a large degree be analyzed in an interesting way in terms of Daniel Dennett's intentional system theory of the mind (Dennett, 1971; 1976). Let me outline the main points of this analysis.

Dennett (1978, p. xxii) defines the concept of a rational, self-conscious person — actually the concept of a self, in light of the above-mentioned terminological question — as the concept of a higher-order intentional system:

> ... persons can be defined as a particular subclass of intentional systems, 'higher order' intentional systems with the capacity for natural language and (hence) consciousness in the fullest sense [self-consciousness].

From this definition it would appear that the class of persons is a subdivision of the class of intentional systems. What, then, are intentional systems?

Dennett's theory of intentional systems is a general theory of explaining *behaviour* from the third-person point of view. If the behaviour of an entity X can be rationally interpreted on the basis of 'the intentional stance', then X is an intentional system. To formulate it differently, if X's behaviour can be rationally described, explained and predicted using intentional predicates, then X is *ipso facto* an intentional system. The category of intentional predicates is a sub-category of Strawsonian P-predicates, namely P-predicates with propositional content or P-predicates which ascribe propositional attitudes, such as beliefs and desires. Accordingly, on the assumption that X is a rational system, X's behaviour can be understood by ascribing to X intentional predicates such as 'X believes that p' and 'X desires that p'. This technical notion of an intentional system X is an *abstract and instrumentalist* notion in the sense that intentional predicates are ascribed to X in abstraction from X's internal constitution and without regard to the fact that X does or does not really have propositional attitudes. From this it follows that Dennett's intentional theory of behaviour is extremely 'liberal', since not only persons but also animals (e.g., dogs), machines (e.g., computers) and even plants (e.g., orchards) can be intentional systems, though of a lower order.

In other words, being an intentional system is a necessary but not a sufficient condition for personhood. What is it, then, that makes an intentional system a *personal* intentional system? The specific difference distinguishing persons from other intentional systems lies in the fact that *complex* intentional predicates must also be ascribed to persons. In order to be able to interpret a person's bodily behaviour — and speech acts — intentional predicates of at least the second order must be ascribed to these intentional systems. Such complex intentional predicates, like 'X has the belief that X has the belief that p' and 'X desires that X desires that p', exhibit the capacity for self-consciousness — *mental reflexivity* — and are constitutive of higher-order intentional systems. As opposed to other, lower-order intentional systems, persons or selves as higher-order intentional systems can take an intentional standpoint with regard to themselves.

A rational, self-conscious person — a self — is a higher-order intentional system, in other words a reflexive system of beliefs and desires. This system can be conceptually divided into a cognitive subsystem on the one hand and a conative subsystem on the other: the domain of beliefs — reason — on one side and the domain of desires — the will — on the other. My view of the problem of the self is that the moral and existential essence of a person — the self of the person in a strict sense — belongs not so much to the domain of true knowledge but to the domain of *free will*. The most important and problematic reflexive structure of the mind of a person is not his intellectual structure, but rather his volitional or motivational structure. We care more about our will than about our reason. We are most interested in the most problematic aspect of our lives: the actions and motives of others and of ourselves. Or to put it metaphorically: the seat of the self is not the head but the heart.

As a consequence, the problem of the self, on this view, coincides with the problem of the freedom of the will, self-determination or personal autonomy. Addressing the question 'What constitutes the self?' amounts to the same thing as taking up the question 'Wherein does personal autonomy consist?'

The hierarchical model of personal autonomy

By turning Plato's analogy between the soul and the city-state upside down, the property of autonomy in modern philosophy has been transferred from political to personal entities. Although there are different models on offer in contemporary analytical anthropology, I shall concentrate on only one particularly influential model. This so-called 'hierarchical' model of personal autonomy — which I wish to discuss critically here — is rooted in the analytical philosophy of freedom espoused by Harry Frankfurt and Gerald Dworkin, and is accordingly also called the 'Frankfurt/Dworkin' model. Bearing in mind the distinction between free action and free will, or in other words that between alternative possibilities and self-determination (Watson, 1987), the problem of personal autonomy amounts to that of free will or self-determination. Not the negative freedom, but the positive freedom of a person is at stake. Frankfurt gives a compatibilist account of free will that starts from a hierarchical analysis of the concept of the conative self (person) and Dworkin explicitly grafts his definition of autonomy onto the same hierarchical analysis of free will. In this section I will set forth the main tenets of this Frankfurt/Dworkin model of personal autonomy.

As said in the previous section, the concept of a person is the concept of an intentional system with the capacity for self-consciousness. Persons necessarily have the capacity for mental reflexivity. Ontological issues apart, the essence of a person can best be understood as a reflexive structure of beliefs, desires and other propositional attitudes. So typical for persons is not only their cognitive and conative structure, but also the reflexive structure of their minds. Now the most important reflexive mental part of persons is, to repeat, not so much their intellectual make-up as their motivational or volitional one. In daily life we are more concerned about our volitional capacity than our ratiocinative one. We are, that is, most engrossed in what is in a sense the most worrying and challenging dimension of our lives: what we (should) do and why we do it.

Frankfurt conceptualizes this range of phenomena about persons in terms of a model that is based on the notion of a *hierarchy of volitions* (Frankfurt, 1971; 1987). The concept of a reflexive will which this notion entails is most innocuous since nothing more is meant by volitions than effective desires (wants, preferences or pro-attitudes), desires that move a person all the way to action. A volition in this sense is not some mysterious act of the mind, but a motive which can be readily attributed to a person to explain his behaviour. The reflexivity of the will is formally modelled by the distinction between first-order and second-order desires. Persons typically not only have desires of the first order, X desires that p, but also desires of the second order, X desires or does not desire that X desires that p. For example, an unhappy smoker does not want to be motivated by his craving for a cigarette: he desires not to desire to smoke. Desires of the first order take actions as their objects, while those of the second order are about first-order desires. It is this conative mode of the capacity for mental reflexivity which Frankfurt (1971, p. 12) deems essential to the life of the person:

> It is my view that one essential difference between persons and
> other creatures is to be found in the structure of a person's will.
> ... No animal other than man, ... appears to have the capacity
> for reflective self-evaluation that is manifested in the formation
> of second-order desires.

The essential capacity of persons to form second-order desires can be seen as their capacity for either *self-evaluation* or *self-identification*. The will of a person is always constituted by such and such a pattern of first-order desires. If a person is concerned about his will, then he critically examines whether or not this or that desire of the first order should be effective. This formation of second-order desires comes to the same thing as the holding of evaluative attitudes towards one's own first-order desires. By taking a positive second-order attitude towards a first-order desire, one also makes this desire more truly 'one's own'. If a person holds a positive attitude of a higher order towards a desire of a lower order, then he identifies himself with this lower-order desire. By adopting a negative stance towards a first-order desire, one also withdraws oneself from this desire, although in a literal sense it is still one's own. If a person holds a negative attitude of a higher order towards a desire of a lower order, then he rejects this lower-order desire — it does not belong any more to his true identity. So if a person consents to a first-order desire, then he identifies himself with it, whereas if a person disallows a first-order desire, then he withdraws himself from it:

> The ... [person] identifies himself, ... through the formation of
> a second-order volition, with one rather than with the other of
> his conflicting first-order desires. He makes one of them more
> truly his own and, in so doing, he withdraws himself from the
> other. (Frankfurt, 1971, p. 18)

Now the personality or character of a person can be interpreted as a particular pattern of desires as this is conceived within the hierarchical model (Williams, 1976). This means that the process of self-identification constitutes a character in the light of an ego-ideal or a self-conception that a person has of himself. Depending on what kind of person he wants to be, a person accordingly tries not only to induce new desires but also to amplify, weaken or eliminate old, already existing desires. Through this process the ultimate goal of self-realization is eventually reached, a goal which is of primordial importance to an autonomous person.

In terms of Frankfurt's analysis, then, a person exercises freedom of will when he acts upon the will or first-order desires he wants to have. If there is a conformity of his first-order desires to his second-order desires, then he enjoys freedom of will. If, on the contrary, there exists a discrepancy between his first-order and second-order desires, then he lacks such a freedom. So free will is volitional harmony, lack of it disharmony. From this hierarchical account of the concept of a person and his free will Dworkin's explicit hierarchical analysis of the concept of personal autonomy follows

90

quite naturally. As indicated by the etymology of the term, 'autos' (self) and 'nomos' (rule or law), two basic threads are closely knit together in the concept of personal autonomy or self-government. Firstly, the government of the person by the person *himself.* This comes close to the issue of self-identification or the formation of character. The person creates himself by identifying himself with his lower-order desires. Secondly, the *government* of the person by the person himself. This relates to the issue of self-evaluation or self-rule. The person rules himself by evaluating his lower-order desires according to his own higher-order desires.

Although the processes of self-identification and self-evaluation are necessary conditions for personal autonomy, they are not sufficient. It is possible that these processes in their very implementation are influenced by circumstances or other people in a way that radically interferes with *personal* autonomy. Identification and evaluation of oneself 'under the influence' of, say, drugs or charismatic leadership would evidently distort self-rule. The procedures by which a person identifies or evaluates himself need to be independent in order to be constitutive of his personal autonomy. When a person rules himself, he must be independent on two fronts. On the one hand he must be independent from the influence of so-called 'alien forces' and on the other hand he must be independent from other people's impact. A person can be called autonomous only if he is not alienated from himself, neither on the natural side by physical causes or blind drives nor on the social side by other people's opinion. When a person acts in an autonomous way, he does not act upon a desire which he rejects or would reject, nor does he act vicariously.

Now all these elements come together in Dworkin's formula for personal autonomy in terms of, firstly, *authenticity* (that is to say, second-order identification / evaluation) and secondly, *procedural independence* (that is to say, the independent status of both processes):

> The full formula for autonomy, then, is authenticity plus procedural independence. A person is autonomous if he identifies with [evaluates] his desires, goals, and values, and such identification [evaluation] is not influenced in ways which make the process of identification [evaluation] in some way alien to the individual. (Dworkin, 1981, p. 61)[1]

1. In his later work Dworkin (1988, pp. 15-18) has weakened the condition of authenticity: it is not so much identification (or evaluation) as *reflection as such* that is crucial to being autonomous. This seems to me to imply far too formal a notion of autonomy, hardly distinguishable from that of self-consciousness in general. I would, therefore, maintain this stronger condition of authenticity and, thus, this more substantial notion of autonomy.

91

Strictly speaking, this means that uncontrollable contingencies and other people's impact will always have the property of alienation. As against this extremely autonomous view I contend, firstly, that the process of self-identification cannot entirely be rooted in autonomous 'acts of the will', and secondly, that the process of self-evaluation depends in an important sense on the normative impact of other people's attitudes.

Self-identification, decision and volitional necessity

One of the most notoriously troublesome aspects of the hierarchical model of personal autonomy is the possibility of an infinite regress (Friedman, 1986; Christman, 1989). A brief sketch of this difficulty is necessary here, as it pertains to the process of self-identification by which desires are made internal (autonomous) or external (heteronomous). As pointed out above, whether a person identifies himself with or withdraws himself from a certain desire depends on whether or not he desires this desire to be his will. This means that the internality or externality of first-order desires is given an explanation by appealing to the formation of second-order desires. However, in its turn an attitude of the second order must be an attitude which belongs truly to the person himself since an external attitude cannot confer an internal status on a desire of the first order. This gives rise to the question of how the internal status of a second-order attitude itself is constituted. If yet further and higher attitudes have to be invoked to determine the internality of second-order attitudes, then an infinite regress seems to be inevitable. If no other attitudes come into play, then it remains on this hierarchical account completely inexplicable how a second-order attitude could be internal at all. This is the so-called *ab initio* problem: how can a higher-order attitude then be internal or autonomous to begin with?

Frankfurt himself has acknowledged this fundamental difficulty, but in order to avoid it he has attempted to explain the process of self-identification by appealing to the notion of decision or decisive commitment (1971; 1976; 1987). Frankfurt claims that a decision is not further susceptible to externality and accordingly, by its *intrinsic* internality, cuts off the possible proliferation of levels. An act of deciding is of necessity internal since deciding is something that one does to oneself. If the commitment of a person is decisive or made without reservation, then it resounds endlessly throughout the possible series of higher orders. Hence, once a person has made up his mind decisively, no further questions about higher-order endorsement are pertinent.

Although it seems possible to come to terms with the difficulty of increasingly higher orders by relying upon the notion of decision, this notion itself is fraught with difficulties of its own. Besides the obscure nature of an act of deciding, the most important difficulty is that the explanation of self-identification by an appeal to acts of deciding entails that self-identification is thought of as a fully *active* process. A person is active with regard to his identifications because his acts of deciding by which he makes some desires truly his own are themselves intrinsically internal. Moreover, the making of a decision amounts to the formation of an intention which is necessarily an activity of the person himself. Making a decision is, according to Frankfurt, above all other mental acts the act of a full-blown autonomous person: '... the person, in making a decision by which he identifies with a desire, *constitutes himself.*' (Frankfurt, 1987, p. 170)

However, the process of self-identification seems to have, at least partially, a *passive* nature. It would be an illusion to think that a person has full voluntaristic control of his identifications, and that what constitutes a person most deeply is subjected to his autonomous will. The influence of acts of the will, such as decisions, on identifications is often weak, and by and large ineffectual. Moreover, deep identifications seem to elude the conscious image a person has of himself. One can very well decide to become a certain sort of character, and yet, notwithstanding one's acts of will, still remain the same sort of character one has always been. A decision to identify oneself only creates an intention to make some desire more truly one's own. If another internal but conflicting desire turns out to be predominant, then one's decision was not wholehearted. However, this failure of wholeheartedness does not indicate of necessity a lack of will-power or sincerity, since the 'heart' of a person may be located in something that is beyond his conscious and voluntaristic control.

This fundamental criticism gives rise to an altogether different view of the nature of self-identification. Surprisingly, this alternative account can also be found in Frankfurt's philosophical work on the nature of the person and his free will. Equally surprisingly, perhaps, this line of his thinking on the topic of personal autonomy and authenticity has not received the attention that it deserves. It is, therefore, worth emphasizing that Frankfurt's thinking on these matters exhibits a considerable tension between two opposite views of the process of self-identification: a more active as against a more passive view. On the one hand, Frankfurt explicitly favours an analysis of self-identification in terms of acts of deciding; but on the other hand, he implicitly develops an analysis of self-identification by appealing to the notion of *caring about something* (Frankfurt, 1982). According to the first view identification is thought of as a second-order attitude and an active process, while according to the second view it is thought of as a first-order attitude and a passive process. Of these two sorts of identification, first-order caring about something seems far more fundamental than decisive second-order commitment or endorsement. The process of caring about something is not only immune to the difficulty of an infinite regress because it belongs to the first-order, it is, paradoxically, also *constitutive* of true authenticity or personal autonomy in a moderated sense.[2] Although passivity is commonly treated as incompatible with autonomy, first-order identification provides the essential limits of the will which are necessary for authentic personal liberation. I now try to substantiate these claims by pointing out some of the fundamental characteristics of the concept of caring about something.

This concept is not so much ethical as it is anthropological. Ethics in a strict sense relates to our dealings with other people, while in caring about something we ourselves are primarily involved. When we care about something, it's about *us*, our own personal projects and ideals or certain individuals and groups to which we are particularly attached. These objects of care are of a more personal kind in the sense that they give some sort of guidance to a caring person in what he does with his own life. How a caring person leads his own life is to a great extent guided by such objects of care as, for example, a professional career, a family tradition, a dear friendship, a political party or a religious community.

Caring about something is not only a personal matter, but also a long-term process and a non-voluntaristic affair. Its temporal as well as volitional structure differs considerably from that of such acts of the will as choosing and deciding. To make a decision, for example, only takes a short period of time, while to care about something lasts for a more or less extended period of time, even for a lifetime. Now if the guidance which is given to a caring person is seen in the light of the temporal extension of his caring, then it becomes understandable why his caring about something can be constitutive of his continuing identity through time. If a person cares about some particular object, then he will integrate his life and conduct more fully around this leading object of his care:

> The moments in the life of a person who cares about something, ..., are not merely linked inherently by formal relations of sequentiality. The person necessarily binds them together, and in the nature of the case also construes them as being bound together, in richer ways. This both entails and is entailed by his own continuing concern with what he does with

---

2. My use of the term 'authenticity' has nothing to do with Dworkin's condition of authenticity in his full formula of personal autonomy. On my alternative view, authenticity comprises passive self-identification as well as social self-evaluation.

himself and with what goes on in his life. (Frankfurt, 1982, pp. 83-84)

This long-term guidance relates intrinsically to the non-voluntarism or the passivity of caring about something, its most fundamental characteristic.

What a person cares about is far more constitutive of the fundamental character of his will than his decisions and other voluntaristic acts. In his caring about something a person feels the influence of a strange kind of necessity in virtue of which his caring is not altogether under his voluntary control. He feels that he cannot help caring so much about this or that as he does. He feels that he cannot bring himself to will otherwise than he does. To refer to this kind of necessity which pertains to what a person's will truly is, Frankfurt (1982, p. 86) uses the term *'volitional necessity'*.[3] The necessity of the will is neither of a logical nor of a causal kind (the latter being typical for the volitional structure of, say, a drug addict). If a person acts upon some first-order desire which is constrained by volitional necessity, then although this person could have acted otherwise if he had decided to do so, he finds himself unwilling to oppose this constraining desire and therefore he is unwilling to act otherwise than he does. This person lacks not so much the power to act otherwise as the will to alter the will he has. It is in this predicament, according to Frankfurt, that the reformer Martin Luther at the Diet in Worms (1521), out of his caring about a particular religious ideal, famously proclaimed: 'Here I stand; *I can do no other;* so help me God, Amen.' Enthralled by a particular volitional necessity, a person is unwilling to act otherwise than he does because to opt for an alternative course of action is unthinkable for him. It is, however, not so much a brute force as an obscure but intimate necessity in virtue of which this person thinks that other courses of action are unthinkable for him (Frankfurt, 1988a).

A more profitable view of the nature of self-identification emerges, I think, when its nature is first and foremost analyzed in terms of caring about something and volitional necessity. If a person cannot help caring about some object, for example his own family, then he is completely invested in it or fully devoted to it. He is so strongly *identified* with it that he *himself* is affected, for better or for worse, by the contingencies which befall the object of his care. However, because of the fact that his caring about this object is constrained by volitional necessity, his identification with it is a first-order as well as a passive process. He does not decide to identify himself with this or that first-order desire, but he finds that some desire of the first-order is categorically directed towards an object he is devoted to. He does not create his

---

3. Williams (1976, p. 207) uses the term 'categorical desire' to refer to a closely related phenomenon.

fundamental identifications at will, but, on the contrary, such identifications create him. Now these passive identifications of the first order determine the fundamental character of the will and by their constraining nature, they also define the limits of the will. They make up the volitional substance of a person, which partly constitutes his identity. If no limits were to be set to the will of a person by means of his basic identifications, then it would become doubtful whether he could have an authentic character at all, since a limitless will can hardly be expressive of a *particular* character.

Emphasizing this basic form of identification by no means implies a denial of the existence and importance of second-order endorsement (or identification of the second order) and other acts of the will. However, all these acts of the higher order are of a derivative or secondary nature since they are performed against the guiding background of the primitive or primary identifications. Unless a person abandons himself, he cannot abandon his deep identifications. It is because a person is identified with something in which his own nature is at stake that he can find the will-power to make certain decisions and choose certain objects in order to preserve and integrate his own identity according to the guidelines of his identifications. The voluntaristic self-control of a person concerns his pursuit of what really interests him and, thus, the elimination of all divergent obstacles which might stand between him and what he really cares about. This means that the deep identifications of a person are preconditions for his acts of will and not the other way around. Basic identifications give direction to the will without which the reality of the self would dissolve.

Caring about something lays the foundation of the character of the will and this implies that first-order desires which are constrained by volitional necessity shape the essential limits of the will. Such a fundamental passivity of the will is often thought of as diminutive or even destructive of personal autonomy and authenticity. However, the necessity of the will is not the same thing as its weakness. Weakness of the will, indeed, destroys personal autonomy, while, on the contrary, volitional necessity enhances authenticity and strengthens the will. The 'alien force' within the motivational structure has in the two cases an altogether different nature. The weakening force is only brutally external, while the necessitating force is paradoxically not only in a sense external but also internal. Although the force of volitional necessity is imposed involuntarily, this necessity is also *self-imposed*:

> The reason a person does not experience the force of volitional
> necessity as alien or as external to himself, ..., is that it coin-
> cides with — and is, indeed, partly constituted by — desires
> which are not merely his own but with which he actively iden-

96

tifies himself. Moreover, the necessity is to a certain extent self-imposed. (Frankfurt, 1982, p. 88)

Because a person's own nature is involved in his caring about certain objects, he himself endorses certain first-order desires which are not altogether under his voluntary control but which are expressive of his caring about these objects. This second-order endorsement (or identification of the second order) makes it possible to understand both how a first-order desire which is in a sense external to a person can at the same time be internal to him, and how this desire which is constrained by volitional necessity can have a liberating effect on this person. Because of the internality of such a necessitating desire, he is susceptible to the feeling of authenticity which the passivity of his will can give.

Nevertheless, the liberating effect of caring about something stems not so much from the hierarchical structure of the subject as it does from the captivating nature of the object. Yet, as Frankfurt (1982, p. 89) asks: 'How are we to understand the paradox that a person may be enhanced and liberated through being seized, made captive, and overcome?' Let me try to formulate a sensible answer. Without the guidance of an object of his care, a person may well be 'the slave of his passions'. Put into the hands of his natural self-centred desires, which come and go, a person may feel himself diminished in that these capricious desires too often disrupt and disintegrate his identity. Although he freely acts upon desires he wants to be effective, the anarchy of his motivational life may be more an impediment to his authenticity than an essential condition for it. Now if a particular object, such as an ideal of life in his cultural context, not only draws the attention of a person but also seizes and captivates him so that he starts caring about it, then his motivational life really becomes *structured*. This means that central to his care for this object, and therefore to the corresponding desires which are constrained by the volitional necessity of his care, all his other motives will get systematized and ranked. The object of his care, then, provides a liberation *from* his self-centred preoccupations and makes a person free *for* what he really values. Because the captivating object is a precious one for him, it stands in need of this person's caring about it in complex cognitive, affective and volitional ways. In this way a motivational structure that is constrained by volitional necessity makes a person susceptible to especially valuable experiences and really fulfilling states. In light of the distinction between freedom 'from' and freedom 'for', it becomes understandable how a captivating object of care which constrains the will by volitional necessity can have a liberating effect.

So although the necessity of the will entails its passivity, volitional necessity can yield a paradoxical form of liberty. This 'liberating captivity' of the will enhances a person in that it gives him a sense of an integrated identity and of true authenticity. It is after all a quite familiar idea in our tradition that persons are at their best when they are not altogether self-centred. When they let themselves be guided in a selfless way by objects which escape their control, they make themselves susceptible to authentic personal liberation.[4] Paradoxically, one has to lose oneself in order to find one's true self.

Self-evaluation, choice and social dependence

Closely related to the problem I discussed in the previous section is that of the authority which second-order desires apparently have in the hierarchical model of personal autonomy (Thalberg, 1978). The difficulty as it bears upon the process of self-evaluation is this. By taking positive or negative second-order attitudes towards his first-order desires a person assesses and evaluates his motivational system. However, where do these evaluative attitudes get their authoritative or normative power from? Attitudes of the second order are on this model, after all, just like the desires of the first order they evaluate, *simply desires*. Going up one level does not automatically confer an evaluative authority upon desires of the second order; ascending to a higher level only brings in a quantitative but not a qualitative difference in the 'bundle of desires'. It seems that the explanation of self-evaluation in terms of higher-order desires is seriously flawed since desires, of whatever order, of themselves never can have a special normative status. Of course, there can be weak self-assessment in terms of positive or negative higher-order desires, but never strong self-evaluation (Taylor, 1977). The difficulty here is not so much that there is a possibility of a regressive ascent, but rather that nothing about the level of desires gives them any special authority with respect to self-evaluation.

Gary Watson (1975) has brought this difficulty eminently to light and has suggested that in order to meet it a qualitative distinction should be made between desiring and valuing, between a motivational and an independent valuational system. To have an evaluative authority, higher-order attitudes must be grounded in a person's values which cannot be reduced to his desires. Now although Frankfurt never explicitly addresses the difficulty, it is possible to derive from his work a distinction of this kind and also an answer to the subsequent question as to what constitutes a person's valuational system. It is worthwhile doing this briefly because it eventually appears that the

---

4. Frankfurt (1982, pp. 89-91) draws special attention to the liberating power of rationality, love and ideals, all of which imply a certain *selflessness*.

explanation of self-evaluation he implicitly has in mind is intimately related to the existentialist account of this process in terms of a radically free choice.

Frankfurt (1971, p. 19, n. 6; my italics) gives the following succinct analysis of self-evaluation:

> In speaking of the evaluation of his own desires and motives
> ..., a person may be *capricious and irresponsible* in forming his
> second-order volitions and give *no serious consideration* to what
> is at stake. Second-order volitions express evaluations only in
> the sense that they are *preferences.* There is *no essential restriction*
> on the kind of basis, *if any,* upon which they are formed.

This comes close to the existentialist conception of personal autonomy. In his self-evaluation an autonomous person can neither submit himself to a pre-established religious or moral authority nor to any culturally embedded valuational system or whatever. On the existentialist view, when an autonomous person assesses and rules himself, he proceeds upon *self-chosen* values and norms.[5] To be ruled otherwise, in whatever way, would be an abdication from his unalienable right and pre-eminent duty to create his own principles and values. In short, the valuational system of an autonomous person is grounded in his radically free choice.

There is no need to flog a dead horse here. Different authors have sufficiently exposed the untenable nature of the existentialist conception of absolute autonomy which reposes on radically free choice (Taylor, 1977). A brief rehearsal of the main objection to this conception may, however, be useful here. If I am right about the assimilation of Frankfurt's analysis to the existentialist view of self-evaluation, then it follows that higher-order attitudes are expressive of self-chosen values. But these putative evaluative attitudes are really either only *factual* preferences or merely *arbitrary* options. Consequently, a special normative status can never accrue to such attitudes. For if, according to the hypothesis under consideration, there are no prior value-criteria whatsoever by reference to which a radically free choice is made, then such a choice is either based upon the strongest attraction of one preference among other alternatives or made without regard to preferences at all. A radically free choice is, after all, just a wanton movement of the mind without any special authority. Here autonomy collapses into *anomy* and, thus, the initial problem of evaluative authority arises again.

The hierarchical model of personal autonomy, at least in Frankfurt's version of it, still contains the supposition that a person's values emerge from

---

5. The *locus classicus* of this existentialist freedom in terms of radically free choice is, of course, Jean-Paul Sartre in, for example, 1948.

his own activity such as choosing in a radically free way. However, to suppose that the normative standard of self-evaluation can be found within the autonomous person himself leads into a blind alley. It is therefore plausible to conjecture, I think, that the valuational system of a person must in an important sense be dependent on the valuational system of the *community* to which he belongs.[6] This is to say that the evaluative judgement which a person makes about his own motivation and conduct hinges in a vital way upon the evaluative judgement which *other people* make about this person's intention and action in the light of their common value-system. This social value-system consists of the authoritative principles, rules, values and norms which are expressive of the normative conception of the good life. Hence, the process of self-evaluation in its procedure cannot be independent, but must be socially dependent. Self-evaluation does not repose on self-chosen values, but is grounded in a given set of social norms and common principles. Although social dependence is usually regarded as incompatible with personal autonomy, such an 'other-directedness' is often not so much an alienating influence as a *constitutive* factor in the true evaluation of the self by itself. The dependence of self-evaluation on social normative standards is paradoxically a requirement for an appropriate sense of personal worth. I myself am promoted by other human beings.

I will now try to complete my case for this moderately heteronomous view by giving a brief account of the social dependence of self-evaluation in terms of the desire for recognition by other people and the social self, and by simultaneously confronting this account with my earlier remarks on caring about something.

If a person cares about something, then he, of course, also values what he cares about. He is interested in the value of what he cares about because this value of the things with which he is so deeply identified determines his own personal worth. However, whether or not a person cares about things which are worth caring about is, if the foregoing argument is correct, not a matter of which he can judge autocratically. The solitary person cannot be the single source of value-judgements about the objects of his care (his basic identifications). His evaluative judgement must, therefore, be informed by the evaluative judgement which other people make about the objects of his care.

6. The idea that the untenable nature of radical autonomy and individualistic self-chosen values leads directly to the plausibility of the community view of self-evaluation will presumably come under attack. If one sees an intrinsic connection between autonomy and *rationality* in a Kantian fashion, then one can try to solve the problem of authority in self-evaluation by an appeal to the isolated 'autonomous rational person' without invoking the community considerations. For an ingenious solution along these lines, see Piper (1985). Although I am aware of this important and classical objection, I will not take it up here as I limit myself in this book to the critical discussion not of the Kantian conception but of the hierarchical conception of personal autonomy.

Only under such circumstances can what a person thinks of himself be a public reality and not a mere private illusion.

Now the dependence of a person's self-evaluation on other people's assesssment is represented in this person's motivational system by his *desire for social recognition* of his identifications. The satisfaction of this desire has a very peculiar nature (Elster, 1978, pp. 70-76). This is so because social recognition is only valuable if it is given by other people who are independent and who are willing to give it. A person cannot force someone else to recognize him because he cannot have both the satisfaction which his manipulation of the other person could give and the satisfaction which the other person's recognition could give. He might as well applaud himself. In seeking the recognition of his personal worth, a person must implicitly recognize the other as a worthy person as well. Jon Elster (1978, p. 73) explains this peculiarity by contrasting recognition with acknowledgement or (aesthetic) appreciation:

> The concept of recognition differs from such related notions as acknowledgement or appreciation in that what is recognized is not the existence or some aesthetic aspect of the person, but his moral worth. By seeking recognition one implicitly recognizes the moral worth of the person from whom recognition is forthcoming, but in seeking appreciation one does not implicitly appreciate the aesthetic value of the person by whom one is to be appreciated. This is so because moral competence *is* moral worth. To recognize someone as morally competent — as I implicitly do when seeking his recognition of my moral worth — is to recognize him as morally worthy as well. Aesthetic competence, on the other hand, does not in any way imply that the competent person also has aesthetic value.

As a consequence, the other person from whom recognition is asked, is an *uncontrolled* source of evaluative judgements about the identifications of a person who asks for recognition. In his search for other people's recognition, a person wants to risk the possible denial of their recognition which follows from their independence. A person is, thus, only interested in other people's assessment of himself if their estimation is not altogether under his voluntary control. This means that the desire for social recognition is a *passive* state of mind. However, this passivity nevertheless seems to be a necessary condition for the constitution of a person's true self-evaluation and his personal worth.

Adam Smith (1759, part III, chap. I, par. 2) wrote:

101

We can never survey our own sentiments and motives, we can never form any judgment concerning them; unless we remove ourselves, as it were, from our own natural station, and endeavour to view them as at a certain distance from us. But we can do this in no other way than by endeavouring to view them with the eyes of other people, or as other people are likely to view them. Whatever judgment we can form concerning them, accordingly, must always bear some secret reference, either to what are, or to what, upon a certain condition, would be, or to what, we imagine, ought to be the judgment of others.

In the same spirit, William James (1892, p. 162) said: 'A man's social me is the recognition which he gets from his mates.' Charles Horton Cooley (1902, p. 184) added to this observation:

A social self of this sort might be called the reflected or looking-glass self ... . A self-idea of this sort seems to have three principal elements: [i] the imagination of our appearance to the other person; [ii] the imagination of his judgment of that appearance, and [iii] some sort of self-feeling, such as pride or mortification.

The formation of a person's evaluative judgement of the things he cares about and his corresponding motivational system can, I think, adequately be understood in terms of this self-idea. By mirroring himself in 'the eyes of his fellow-men', a person evaluates himself; by confronting himself in reality as well as in his imagination with the judgement of other people, a person judges himself. To show this I will offer a concise commentary on the three elements mentioned in Cooley's idea of the social self as the reflected or looking-glass self, which together constitute the process of self-evaluation.

In the first place, the presentation of the self: a person, motivated by his desire for recognition, displays in his words and deeds the things he cares about to other people. Of course, a person does not present his 'appearance' or identifications hazardously to all the world and his wife. It would, indeed, be very unwise to put one's fame and fortune as, for example, an intellectual in the hands of the grocer around the corner. A person's self-presentation, therefore, contains a reference to *qualified* other persons and even to *potential* other persons such as future generations. However, in order to preserve his sanity and to keep away from self-deception, a person must ask for recognition by other people who do not postpone their judgement indefinitely and who are willing to give a well-informed, as well as an independent, judgement. So even if a person controls, in some sense, the social reference of his self-presentation and self-evaluation, this person's control will still be limited by the passive nature of his demand for recognition.

Subsequently, the pro- and contra-attitudes of the others: a person takes towards his own identifications the evaluative attitudes of other people which they form concerning his presented identifications. By adopting the social appraisal of the things he cares about, a person evaluates himself. If a person distances himself from his own motivational system in order to assess it, then he reflectively looks at his motives through 'the eyes of other people'. A person's positive and negative attitudes of the second order are implicitly the evaluative attitudes of other people. The self-image of a person is the reflected image of him in the mind of other people.

This is not to say that a person's evaluative judgement of himself just depends on nothing more than the evaluative judgement which one particular other person or even a certain group of qualified other persons makes about him. His self-evaluation reposes neither on a conventional assent nor on an absolute standard. The valuational system of a person is grounded in the evaluative authority of what George Herbert Mead has called '*the generalized other*':

> The organized community or social group which gives to the individual his unity of self may be called 'the generalized other'. The attitude of the generalized other is the attitude of the whole community. (Mead, 1934, p. 154)[7]

In their evaluation of the things a person cares about, concrete other persons do not express their idiosyncratic values, but the value-system of the community as a whole. This highest court of appeal has a special normative status because it *transcends* the person's evaluative judgement of himself as well as the other person's evaluative judgement of him. Let it be clear that by a transcendent valuational system I do not mean an absolute or separated value-system in a Platonic sense. Rather, what I have in mind are notions such as 'the conversation of mankind' (Oakeshott, 1959) and 'a form of life' (Wittgenstein, 1953) in so far as these notions pertain to common principles, rules, values and norms which are neither fully immanent nor strongly transcendent. They both refer to an inherited tradition of valuing to which both the person who asks for recognition and the other persons who give or deny it are subordinated. So even if a person can be critical of an evaluative judgement of his identifications by a particular (group of) other person(s) and

---

7. Akin to this idea of the generalized other is Adam Smith's notion of 'the impartial spectator'.

even if he sometimes must resist this judgement, his self-evaluation will ultimately still bear a reference to this background of valuing — to the generalized other.

And last but not least, the self-feeling: by taking the evaluative attitudes of other people towards him, a person's self-judgement produces certain self-feelings and reactive attitudes towards himself. These personal affections derived from the valuations of others, which Gabriele Taylor (1985) has called 'emotions of self-assessment' such as pride, shame and guilt, determine a person's self-esteem and reveal his personal worth. If the opinion of others is positive, a person feels enhanced, while in those cases that it is negative he feels debased.

If all turns out well, a person can as a result of his socially evaluated self-presentation be affected by especially valuable emotions. An affection such as pride gives him a sense of personal strength. Because of its appropriate social reference, the pride a person takes in the things he cares about expresses true personal worth. So although self-evaluation is not procedurally independent, it reveals the true value of the self. Socially dependent self-evaluation thus constitutes authentic self-assessment. Paradoxically, one has to look in 'the eyes of the other' in order to see the true value of oneself.

Autonomy and caring about oneself

I suggested some amendments of the notions of self-identification and self-evaluation which are pivotal to the hierarchical model of personal autonomy. Instead of relying on such 'acts of the will' as decision and choice for the explanation of self-identification and self-evaluation, I stressed the non-voluntaristic as well as the non-individualistic character of these processes by invoking the notions of volitional necessity and social dependence. Volitional necessity in the first process generates *passive* self-identification, while dependence on other people in the second one gives rise to *social* self-evaluation. However, as I have argued, the existence of these 'alienating influences' in these processes decisively damages the credibility of the concept of extreme personal autonomy: passive self-identification as well as social self-evaluation are incompatible with the 'stability' of personal autonomy. My constructive criticism of the Frankfurt/Dworkin model of personal autonomy has, therefore, the consequence that this extremely autonomous view must be replaced by a moderately autonomous view or, what comes to the same thing, a *moderately heteronomous* view of personal autonomy. For this reason I propose, accordingly, to substitute the concept of extreme personal autonomy by that of *caring about oneself*. In my moderately heteronomous view, both elements, passive self-identification and social self-evaluation, come together in the concept of a person who cares about himself.

Although the moderately heteronomous view of personal autonomy seems to go against the grain of dominant contemporary analytical thinking about the topic, such a view is nevertheless not at all surprising. My view of personal autonomy, and my analytical anthropology in general, firmly belong to one of the mainstreams of Western philosophy. Martha Nussbaum in her *The Fragility of Goodness* (1986, p. 20) roughly distinguishes between two types of practical rationality. Type *A*, of which Plato developed one version, comprises amongst other things the theses that the person is fully active and that the goal of practical reasoning consists of uninterrupted control as well as the total elimination of external influences. Though not completely orthogonal, type *B*, of which Aristotle formulated one version, includes amongst other things the theses that the person is also passive or receptive and that practical reasoning aims at the balance between control and risk; according to this second type, practical reason is directed towards the good life in a world where external forces also have their influence. Rendered metaphorically, type *A* represents the 'Apollonian' view, type *B* the 'Dionysian' view of practical rationality (Blackburn, 1998, p. 88).

In terms of this classification, my view of personal autonomy, and my broader analytical anthropology, undoubtedly belong to the Dionysian type *B*. The basic idea behind this type of analytical anthropology is the inescapable *vulnerability* of human beings. If a person cares about himself as identified with certain things and if he takes seriously other people's estimation of his identifications, then he is a vulnerable man. Because neither his personal authenticity nor his personal worth are altogether under his volitional control, the fate and fortune of a caring person is in a sense a matter of good or bad luck. The passive dimension of human life opens up not only the possibility of inner conflict and tragedy but also that of authentic self-realization and happiness. What a person cares about can be the uncontrollable source of calamity as well as ecstasy. This does not mean, however, that my analytical anthropology leads to a kind of pessimism or fatalism; it only means that we are not the extremely autonomous authors of ourselves in the sense of self-creation by fiat. In my Dionysian, analytical anthropology the stability of personal autonomy is, for that reason, changed for the fragility of caring about oneself.

Chapter Five

Frankfurt on the Nature of the Will

Introduction

In the previous chapter, while critically discussing the hierarchical Frankfurt/Dworkin model, I already roughly sketched the contours of my own alternative view of personal autonomy. In the last two chapter of this book, I will further work out the two basic claims of this moderately heteronomous view. The first claim was that the process of self-identification cannot entirely be rooted in autonomous acts of the will such as decision and choice, and the second claim was that the process of self-evaluation depends in an important sense on the normative impact of other people's attitudes. In this chapter, I want to elaborate further the first element of my moderately heteronomous view, namely passive self-identification. To that end, I give an interpretation of Harry Frankfurt's theory of the will with respect to the complementary issues of autonomy and necessity. So I shall run again through the basic tenets of Frankfurt's hierarchical model of personal autonomy and place them in a broader context to deepen my position.

Frankfurt's theory of the will pertains to the philosophy of free will (or personal autonomy) rather than to the philosophy of intentional action. Accordingly, his theory should not be confused with 'volitionalism' in action theory which holds, roughly, that a bodily movement is an intentional action if and only if it is caused by a volition. Now, as I see it, Frankfurt's theory of the will, as a theory about the nature and structure of the will, is *complex*. My central claim is that he actually brings *three distinct conceptions* of the will into play without ever explicitly distinguishing them from one another. My first task here is then to make explicit these conceptions and to justify the tripartite distinction made. Although my discussion will be limited to Frankfurt's view of the nature and structure of the will, this distinction, and the points made about its components, can easily be generalized. In my opinion, such a tripartite distinction must form an essential part of any rich theory of the will. In view of this distinction I then shall return to my claim about passive self-identification. My moderately heteronomous theory of personal identity can partly be spelled out as the combination of a hybrid thesis about the concept of personal autonomy with an asymmetrical dependency thesis, according to which active self-identification depends upon passive self-identification, but not vice versa. The combination of these two theses constitutes what I call the doctrine of *volitional foundationalism*. Let me now start first with distinguishing the three conceptions in Frankfurt's overall theory of the will.

Three conceptions of the will distinguished

Reading Frankfurt in order to get an answer to the question 'What is the will?' is *prima facie* bewildering. On a first, critical reading, Frankfurt seems to be inconsistent and even to contradict himself. On a second, charitable reading, however, one discovers that Frankfurt's usage of the term 'will' is ambiguous between three meanings. That is to say, Frankfurt's employment of the concept of the will is *equivocal*. This is not without importance since Frankfurt's equivocation in the end, as I will try to show in the last section, turns out to be explanatory of the perhaps surprising fact that his theory of personal autonomy is not only partly in line with the extremely autonomous view but also partly in accord with my moderately heteronomous view of the matter. But to begin with, I shall distinguish between three distinct conceptions of the will so as to disambiguate his usage of the term 'will' and, consequently, to make for coherent reading. In this section, I will extensively quote Frankfurt to localize these utterly different employments of the concept of the will and to clearly bring out the tripartite distinction which I propose to make.

In constructing a theory of the will Frankfurt initially favours the Hobbes-Hume tradition as against the Kantian one.[8] He endorses Hume's principle that 'reason is, and ought only to be, the slave of the passions, and can never pretend to any other office than to serve and obey them' (Hume, 1739-1740, p. 415), that is to say, reason is neither normatively nor motivationally practical. As a result, the most distinctive feature of human nature resides, according to Frankfurt, not in reason but in the most personal and the more intimate faculty of *the will*. Moreover, Frankfurt entirely agrees with Hobbes's reduction of the will to the bundle of appetites or desires. So the first conception or what I call the 'appetitive' will is then defined by him in this way:

> To identify an agent's will is either to identify the desire (or desires) by which he is motivated in some action he performs or to

8. Important representatives of the Kantian tradition are, for example, Wolf (1990) and Korsgaard (1996).

identify the desire (or desires) by which he will or would be motivated when or if he acts. An agent's will, then, is identical with
one or more of his first-order desires. But the notion of the will,
as I am employing it, is not coextensive with the notion of first-
order desires. It is not the notion of something that merely in-
clines an agent in some degree to act in a certain way. Rather, it is
the notion of an *effective* desire — one that moves (or will or
would move) a person all the way to action. Thus the notion of
the will is not coextensive with the notion of what an agent in-
tends to do. For even though someone may have a settled intention to do X, he may nonetheless do something else instead of
doing X because, despite his intention, his desire to do X proves
to be weaker or less effective than some conflicting desire.
(Frankfurt, 1971, p. 14)

Surprisingly at first glance, Frankfurt outlines a totally different conception of the will in his critical discussion of the 'breathtaking' Cartesian thesis
about the freedom of the will, as presented and defended by Rogers Albritton
(1985). This thesis propounds that the will is perfectly, absolutely, unconstrain-
edly and unlimitedly free — the unfreedom of the will is inconceivable. After
trying to make sense of this bold doctrine in terms of the unlimited power
and alternatively the simplicity of the will, Frankfurt concludes that the
Cartesian thesis can be justified, not as a doctrine about the freedom of the
will, but only as a doctrine about its *activity*. So the second conception or
the '*active*' will is conceptualized by him as follows:

... *the will is absolutely and perfectly active.* In other words, there
can be no such thing as a passive willing. All of the movements
of my will — for instance, my choices and decisions — are *movements that I make.* None is a mere impersonal occurrence, in
which my will *moves without my moving it.* None of my choices
or decisions merely happens. Its occurrence *is* my activity, and I
can no more be a passive bystander with respect to my own
choices and decisions than I can be passive with respect to any of
my own actions. It is possible for me to be passive when my arm
rises, but I cannot be passive when I raise it. Now every willing is
necessarily an action; unlike the movements of an arm, it is only
as actions that volitions can occur. Thus, activity is of the essence
of the will. Volition precludes passivity by its very nature.
(Frankfurt, 1989, p. 79)

109

There is, astonishingly perhaps, still another conception of the will at work in Frankfurt's more recent writings that goes beyond the appetitive as well as the active conception. This third conception makes its first appearance in the context of his reflections on the importance of what we care about (Frankfurt, 1982). According to Frankfurt, caring about something exhibits a special kind of necessity, what he calls *volitional necessity*, in virtue of which caring is not altogether under the person's voluntary control. Unthinkability, the counterpart of volitional necessity, is similarly a mode of necessity which constrains or limits the dynamism and organisation of the will. So Frankfurt gives the third conception or the '*substantial*' will the following characterization:

> Unthinkability is a mode of necessity with which the will sometimes binds itself and limits choice. ... The will of a rational agent need not be ... empty or devoid of substantial character. It is not necessarily altogether formal and contentless, having no inherent proclivities of its own. If a person's will were a completely featureless instrument, with no capacity other than to transmute his judgment about what to do into an effective expression of his active powers, then he would closely resemble the 'bare person' to which Rawls says utilitarianism reduces the agent of rational choice. In fact, however, it is precisely in the particular content or specific character of his will — which may salubriously lead him to act against his judgment — that the rationality of person may in part reside. There is a mode of rationality that pertains to the will itself. Like the mode of rationality that is articulated in the necessary truths of logic, it has to do with the inviolability of certain limits. Logical necessities define what it is impossible for us to conceive. The necessities of the will concern what we are unable to bring ourselves to do. (Frankfurt, 1988a, pp. 189-190)

In my judgement, then, at least three conceptions of the will are present in Frankfurt's writings. According to the first, the will is nothing but *effective* desire (of the first order). This appetitive conception is standardly associated with the hierarchical model of personal autonomy, as introduced in the previous chapter. According to the second, the will is synonymous with *act of will* (decision, choice and intention). This active conception is directly connected with what I called voluntaristic or active self-identification. And according to the third, the will is a *faculty* of the mind (the 'motivational organ'). This substantial conception is the one which emerged during my

110

critical discussion of the hierarchical model.

Both the first and the second conception of the will can readily be understood within the scope of the debate on freedom and determinism (necessity) between advocates of compatibilism and those of incompatibilism. The third conception, however, transcends the framework of this classical debate because the autonomy of the third kind of will — the substantial will — *positively requires* necessity. That is to say, autonomy as related to the substantial conception of the will is not only compatible with necessity (or determinism): on this third conception, the former also intrinsically involves the latter. The constitution and autonomy of the substantial will needs the necessities of the will. Although this conception of the will is somewhat unfamiliar and non-standard in the debate, I shall try to show that it captures an all-important fact about our volitional nature — a deep fact which is often overlooked or neglected. In what follows, I shall elucidate each of these conceptions of the will and set forth my reasons for drawing the attendant tripartite distinction.

Desires and the appetitive will

Frankfurt's conception of the appetitive will is, as suggested above, thoroughly Hobbesian. Frankfurt not only, like Hobbes, reduces the will to the bundle of appetites or desires, he also, again like Hobbes, correspondingly rejects the (scholastic) interpretation of the will as the faculty of rational choice and decision. Compare his definition of the will (volition) as 'the notion of an *effective* desire [of the first order] — one that moves (or will or would move) a person all the way to action', with the one that Hobbes (1651, p. 44) gives of the will as the last appetite in deliberating:

> When in the mind of man, Appetites, and Aversions, Hopes, and Feares, concerning one and the same thing, arise alternately; and divers good and evil consequences of the doing, or omitting the thing propounded, come successively into our thoughts; ... the whole summe of Desires, Aversions, Hopes and Fears, continued till the thing be either done, or thought impossible, is that we call DELIBERATION. ... In Deliberation, the last Appetite, or Aversion, immediately adhaering to the action, or to the omission thereof, is that wee call the WILL; the Act, (not the faculty,) of *Willing*. ... The Definition of the *Will*, given commonly by the Schooles, that it is a *Rationall Appetite*, is not good. For if it were, then could there be no Voluntary Act against Reason.

Because the will is neither a substantial faculty nor an active power and because it has no rational nature, willing reduces to pure and simple wanting or desiring 'immediately adhering to the action'. Now this Hobbesian reduction of the will (volition) to effective desire is perfectly suited for the theoretical purposes of compatibilism and naturalized philosophy of mind and action in general. Let me then give more details about Frankfurt's conception of the appetitive will and its relation to personal autonomy as well as to causal necessity (determinism) within the explanatory framework of naturalism and compatibilism.

Although Frankfurt endorses naturalism, he is surely not a proponent of the causal theory of action (Davidson, 1980), according to which beliefs and desires (reasons) causally explain and constitute intentional actions (Frankfurt, 1978). Correspondingly, when desires compete or conflict, he does not appeal to the motivational strength principle to explain what then happens. On this principle, which is central to the causal theory of action, the 'strongest' desire — the desire with the highest degree of causal power to move the agent — always prevails. To spell it out, if an agent wants to do A more than he wants to do B and he believes himself free to do either A or B, then he will intentionally do A if he does either A or B intentionally (Mele, 1992, 46-85). In order to account for what happens in case of a motivational conflict, Frankfurt (1971, pp. 13-16) introduces as an alternative a *hierarchy* of desires, i.e. a model that involves appetitive levels or orders.

As stated by this hierarchical model, first-order desires take actions as their objects; they have the structure 'X desires to perform such-and-such an action'. Some of these first-order desires constitute the will or first-order *volitions*, namely those which are effective in action. Now only persons are, moreover, capable of forming second-order desires and volitions. Second-order desires take first-order desires as their objects; they exhibit the structure 'X desires or does not desire that X desires to perform such-and-such an action'. Some of these second-order desires are second-order *volitions*, namely those concerning first-order desires of which X desires that they are (or will or would become) effective in action. For example, a compulsive liar who, upon reflection, wants to change his character for the better: he desires that he desires to tell the truth. When he actually starts desiring to tell the truth and really tells the truth, his second-order volition will be gratified.

Frankfurt's introduction of hierarchy brings in its wake an extension of his conception of the appetitive will. Besides the will as effective desire or volition of the first order, we now also have the reflective will as second-order volition. In light of this hierarchical Hobbesian will, Frankfurt (1971, p. 18; 1976, pp. 62-66) ingeniously construes the formation of second-order volitions in terms of *self-identification*. A person who desires that a certain

112

desire constitutes (or will or would constitute) his will, identifies himself with it; conversely, he withdraws himself from it when he does not desire to be motivated by such a desire. There is an important sense in which a certain desire with which a person identifies himself is *more truly his own*, whereas another desire from which he withdraws himself is not strictly his own, although the latter desire may still remain part of his ongoing stream of consciousness. Accordingly, in as much as the will constitutes the essence of the self, the higher level volitions are expressive of the 'deep self', while the lower level ones are only expressive of the 'superficial self'.[9]

In dealing with a case of conflicting desires, then, Frankfurt appeals to the identification principle. In such a case, all other things being equal, a person acts upon the desire that is more truly his own than the other desire(s). As a result, it is not true that the strongest of two (or more) conflicting motives always prevails because a person can identify himself with his *weakest* desire. At least sometimes a person apparently does what he wants less. This is not to say that identification invariably succeeds in managing the energies of the will. In spite of his identification with the weakest desire and his effort to counteract the causal power of the strongest desire, a person may fail to eliminate or reduce the effectiveness of the latter in action. In such a case — for example, in the case of the recidivist addict — the person is alienated from himself since he does not possess the will he really wants, and since he also acts contrary to what he really wants. His deplorable predicament can most naturally be described as 'X lacks the will-power or volitional strength' or 'X loses his self-control or autonomy'.

Once the conception of the hierarchical appetitive will and the attendant notion of self-identification are in place, Frankfurt (1971, pp. 20-21) explains the constitution of the *autonomy* of the will by invoking the process of self-identification and the state of volitional harmony. Self-identification with an effective desire of the first order is a necessary and sufficient condition for the desire's autonomy. When first-order volitions are conform to second-order volitions, the will enjoys autonomy; conversely, when first-order volitions are at variance with second-order volitions, it suffers from heteronomy. Accordingly, the self is autonomous if and only if the superficial self harmonizes with the deep self. Now Frankfurt's explication of personal autonomy as volitional harmony has considerable advantages.

For one thing, in contradistinction to Hobbes's crude theory of freedom as doing what one wants, the hierarchical model can, in line with our intuitions, distinguish between the case of ordinary people on the one hand and psychopathological cases such as kleptomaniacs and neurotics on the other.

9. I borrow the term 'deep self' from Wolf, 1987, pp. 50-53.

In a trivial but counter-intuitive sense, the neurotic hand-washer is autonomous because he does what he wants (most) since nothing impedes him from washing his hands the countless times a day his obsessive desire occurs. However, the effective desire to wash his hands is, in a profound sense, heteronomous because it is not endorsed by a second-order volition. The fact that the neurotic's will turns out to be in disharmony is precisely symptomatic of his pathology. The neurotic's superficial self is disconnected from his deep self as it is governed by uncontrollable psychic forces foreign to himself.

Moreover, Frankfurt's hierarchical model provides a plausible compatibilist answer to the classical question 'How is personal autonomy possible, given the biological, psychological and social determination of a person?' It can do this because the process of self-identification and the state of volitional harmony — the necessary and sufficient conditions for personal autonomy — are perfectly compatible with whatever sort of determinism or causal necessitation. To be sure, the thesis of determinism implies the causal necessitation of our desires and volitions. Yet, as long as we also identify ourselves with our desires and volitions, we still are and remain autonomous with regard to these motivations. That is to say, provided that our desires and volitions are also controlled by our deep selves, we keep on having autonomous motives. Furthermore, it is not contradictory to suppose that the process of self-identification and the state of volitional harmony are themselves causally necessitated. The fact that I am determined in the formation of my second-order volitions does not preclude the fact that I am autonomous.

Actually, Frankfurt (1971, p. 25) says that the hierarchical model is *neutral* with respect to the problem of determinism.[10] But, of course, precisely this neutrality (or non-commitment) makes this model straightforwardly compatible with whatever kind of determinism or causal necessitation. It is in this sense that Frankfurt's hierarchical model of personal autonomy is naturalistic — in contrast to, for example, a Kantian theory of noumenal freedom. As maintained by such a naturalistic model, there is no need to go beyond the deterministic or mechanistic world-order to explain the possibility of autonomy. Self-conscious persons simply are *special* mechanisms in that they have the capacity to reflect upon their desires and volitions in a critical way — they can form second-order volitions — and it is upon this capacity alone that their autonomy depends.

10. In this regard, Frankfurt's attitude of neutrality is comparable to Peter Strawson's (1962) attitude of non-commitment to either compatibilism or incompatibilism (libertarianism).

114

Decisions and the active will

On Frankfurt's hierarchical model, the freedom of the self is determined by the deep self. Or, to put it less metaphorically, the autonomy (internality or activity) of first-order desires and volitions is constituted by second-order volitions. Yet, who, or what, determines the freedom of the deep self itself? Desires and volitions of the first order are made autonomous through self-identification; but how is this source of autonomy in its turn made autonomous? Who, or what, constitutes the autonomy of the second-order volitions themselves? Clearly, if a still deeper self has to be posited, or if still higher appetitive or volitional levels have to be introduced, then there looms a *regress* which apparently can only be terminated in an arbitrary way.

Faced with this central difficulty, Frankfurt is at first tempted to say that the deep self's freedom is self-determining, or that the autonomy of second-order volitions is self-constitutive, and to admit candidly that this suggestion indeed has a mysterious ring:

> As for a person's second-order volitions themselves, it is impossible for him to be a passive bystander to them. They *constitute* his activity — i.e., his being active rather than passive — and the question of whether or not he identifies himself with them cannot arise. ... This notion of identification is admittedly a bit mystifying, and I am uncertain how to go about explicating it. In my opinion, however, it grasps something quite fundamental in our inner lives, and it merits a central role in the phenomenology and philosophy of human mentality. (Frankfurt, 1975, p. 54)

However, Frankfurt later explicitly acknowledges that even second-order volitions can be passive and, in an attempt to mitigate the mystery, he proposes to explain identification by an appeal to the notion of *decision* (Frankfurt, 1987, pp. 166-169). In this way he escapes from the regress problem because the autonomy of decision-making is less obscurely self-constitutive than that of second-order volitions. In light of the fact that decisions are *necessarily* internal or active, decisive self-identification will become the keystone in the constitution of personal autonomy. Decisions as intrinsically active can then be the bedrock of the hierarchical model. Why is it that decisions are necessarily active?

Decisions, unlike desires, are not susceptible to passivity; by their nature they are immune to externality. The neurotic hand-washer is a passive bystander to the alien desire to wash his hands. By contrast, the compulsive liar cannot be passive with regard to his decision by which he identifies himself with the desire to tell the truth. Though a person can very well be a passive bystander with regard to some of his desires, he cannot be passive with regard to his decisions. There can be passive desiring, but no passive deciding. Accordingly, whereas an irresistible desire can move a person against his will, a decision is necessarily taken or made by his own will. One simply cannot decide against one's own will. To take a decision is always an action done to oneself. A person may be induced or even coerced to decide or he may take the wrong decision, yet if he *really* decides, then his decision is *fully his own*. To take a decision — to execute an act of will — is to be fully active in making it.

Obviously, it is in the context of the analysis of the nature of decision-making and the role of decisive self-identification in the hierarchical model that we encounter Frankfurt's second conception of the will as 'absolutely and perfectly active'. Taking a decision, like making a choice or forming an intention, is a *pure act* of the will. So the threatening regress problem is dealt with not by introducing more additional levels in the appetitive will, but by resorting to an altogether different conception of the will. Now Frankfurt's conception of the active will is, to my mind, reminiscent of Thomas Reid's conceptualization of the will as the *active power* of self-determination (Reid, 1788, pp. 57-64). By exerting his active power a person autonomously determines his own will. Reid sharply contrasts this power and the acts of that power with the appetites, desires and passions which do not determine the will although they may have an inciting influence upon the determinations of the will by the person himself. He then explicates further this kind of active self-determination of the will in terms of *agent-causation*:

> The name of a *cause* and of an *agent*, is properly given to that being only, which, by its active power, produces some change in itself, or in some other being. The change, whether it be of thought, of will, or of motion, is the *effect*. Active power, therefore, is a quality in the cause, which enables it to produce the effect. And the exertion of that active power in producing the effect, is called *action, agency, efficiency*. (Reid, 1788, p. 268)

According to Reid, the necessary and sufficient conditions for person X to be the agent-cause of volition v — a pure act of the will such as a decision — are the following (Rowe, 1991):[11]

---

11. For a contemporary attempt to make a case for a credible and viable agent-causal theory, see the essays of W.L. Rowe, T. O'Connor and R. Clarke in O'Connor, 1995, pp. 151-215. For a discussion of this rehabilitation project, see Cuypers 1998b.

(1) X is a person that has *power* to bring about *v*,

(2) X *exerts* its power to bring about *v*, and

(3) X has the power *to refrain* from bringing about *v*.

When these conditions are fulfilled, the agent-cause X brings about the effect *v*. The first condition says that active power is a quality possessed by a person or a *substance*. According to Reid, only beings that have will and understanding — i.e., persons — possess active powers and, consequently, only persons can be efficient causes in the original, strict and proper sense. The second condition states that the exercising of active power by the person constitutes action or *activity*. Power and its exertion are necessarily connected, since power that cannot be exerted is no power. So if a person has the power to produce volition *v*, then he necessarily can exert that power. The third condition establishes that the concept of active power includes the *contingency* of activity. If a person really has power to bring about volition *v*, then he also has power *not* to bring it about. The bringing about of *v* is a contingent existence, because it is 'up to the person' whether or not to exert his active powers.

This conception of the will as an active power and the acts of that power — decisions, choices and intentions — inescapably brings in incompatibilism, or at least incompatibilist intuitions. Especially the third condition of agent-causation inevitably turns Reidian volitional self-determination into an incompatibilist doctrine. This is so because the third condition warrants the *robustness* of activity. If a person could not refrain from bringing about volition *v*, he would have been subject to necessity lacking all power. Consequently, the person himself would not have played any active role in the occurrence of *v*. Moreover, the third condition secures the *impossibility* of caused agent-causing or determined self-determination. If a person were caused to agent-cause volition *v*, then he could not have refrained from agent-causing *v*. Because the necessary existence of *v* would violate the requirement of contingent activity, caused agent-causing or determined self-determination is impossible. Hence, since no event or other person can cause a person to agent-cause a volition, he is the *uncaused cause* of that volition. Correspondingly, robustly active or self-determining persons are 'unmoved movers' or 'uncontrolled controllers' or 'undetermined determinators'. That persons themselves are the real originators of their volitions and actions is the single most important principle of the agent-causal theory.

If I am in the right about my assimilation of Frankfurt's conception of the active will to the Reidian agent-causal theory, then it becomes apparent that the hierarchical model of personal autonomy harbours incompatibilist presuppositions. That is to say, if hierarchical autonomy requires decisive identification, and if decisions are pure acts of the will as conceived of in Reidian terms, then it follows that hierarchical autonomy is incompatible with determinism. According to Frankfurt, decisions are 'absolutely and perfectly active' movements of the will and, as stated by the Reidian incompatiblilist view, it is incoherent to claim that these purely active occurrences might be determined or causally necessitated. Let me spell it out. If determinism is true, then decisions are nothing but intermediate links in a deterministic causal chain from environment and motives to actions; their occurrence is then necessitated just like everything else. On the Reidian view, however, a necessary occurrence is a passive occurrence. So the truth of determinism would imply that decisions are passive. Consequently, decisions can only be active in the required sense if their occurrence is not necessitated. The occurence of decisions as 'absolutely and perfectly active' has to be a contingent existence since, on the Reidian view, activity conceptually implies non-necessitation or contingency. So the fact that decisions are purely active occurences implies the falsity of determinism.

Moreover, decisions can only be active in the required sense if their contingent occurrence is not the outcome of chance or luck. If the outcome is an effect of a 'chancy' or 'lucky' process, then the person himself really has *no control* over the outcome. The outcome on every particular occasion just seems then to be like winning the prize in a lottery. A person who lacks control over a process and its outcome is just a passive bystander to that process and he plays no active role whatsoever in the occurence of that outcome. So randomness (chance or luck), like necessity, inevitably entails passivity and, conversely, activity conceptually implies non-randomness or control. As a consequence, to secure the person's active control over his decisions, we cannot but conclude, as maintained by the Reidian agent-causal theory, that the person *directly causes* them. In other words, decisions as purely active occurences are the outcomes of a controlling power of the person who is at liberty to exert that power or not. The person determines his decisions by causing them, whereas he himself remains the undetermined originator or the uncaused cause of them. He himself determines without being determined. So, again, the fact that decisions as 'absolutely and perfectly active' movements of the will are agent-caused implies the falsity of determinism, a thesis at the core of incompatibilism.

Looked upon from the angle of the Reidian agent-causal theory, Frankfurt's hierarchical model of personal autonomy constitutes an interesting attempt to reduce and eliminate the notion of agent-causation within the explanatory framework of compatibilism and naturalism, yet in the end this project of reduction and elimination proves to be *circular* (Velleman, 1992). That is to say, Frankfurt tries to give an account of autonomy and robust activity — i.e., self-determination — in terms of reflective self-identification, but the explanation of *decisive* second-order volitions in the last analysis turns out to *presuppose* the incompatibilist notion of agent-causation. This ineradicable notion makes the prospects for a compatibilist naturalization of autonomy and robust activity very bleak indeed. Autonomy irreducibly requires original, undetermined activity of the person and only agent-causation seems capable of fulfilling this role.

On another look, even apart from incompatiblist presuppositions, the notion of decision itself does not fit well with the Hobbesian-Humean framework of Frankfurt's hierarchical model of personal autonomy. To cut off the proliferation of more and more higher appetitive or volitional levels in a *non-arbitrary* way, decisive self-identification must also be justified. Now this characteristic of decisive second-order volitions seems to be guaranteed because *real* decisions are preceded by a process of deliberation and they are taken for practical reasons. To make a deliberate and reason-based decison seems, therefore, to exclude it from being unwarranted or being arbitrary. So when a person identifies himself decisively, his self-identification is not arbitrary. However, by invoking the notion of a deliberate and reason-based decision to end the regress non-arbitrarily, Frankfurt seems to rely, implicitly at least, on a kind of Kantian *reason view of autonomy* (Wolf, 1990; Korsgaard, 1996). But if the autonomy of the will ultimately depends upon the judgement of reason, then Hume's principle that 'reason is, and ought only to be the slave of the passions' is thereby violated. So by merely appealing to the notion of decision, Frankfurt drifts away from the Hobbesian-Humean framework of his hierarchical model.

Carings and the substantial will

Although the conception of the appetitive will and that of the active will occupy entirely distinct and even mutually exclusive positions in Frankfurt's overall view of the nature and the structure of the will, they are both well-known conceptions in the classical debate between compatibilists and incompatibilists on autonomy and necessity. There is, however, still another conception of the will at work in Frankfurt's (more recent) work that goes beyond the framework of the standard debate: 'Unthinkability is a mode of necessity with which the will sometimes binds itself and limits choice. ... The will of a rational agent need not be ... empty or devoid of substantial character.' According to this rather uncommon conception, necessity *inherently belongs* to the very nature of the will's autonomy. It is not so much that autonomy is extrinsically compatible or, for that matter, incompatible with necessity as that it *intrinsically includes* necessity. That is to say, a particular

119

kind of necessity — namely, volitional necessity — is of the essence of the will's autonomy. The necessities of the will constitute the will's essential character and its autonomy:

> The notion that necessity does not inevitably undermine auton-omy is familiar and widely accepted. But necessity is not only compatible with autonomy; it is in certain respects essential to it. There must be limits to our freedom if we are to have sufficient personal reality to exercise genuine autonomy at all. What has no boundaries has no shape. (Frankfurt, 1988b, p. ix)

Correspondingly, the will as constrained by volitional necessity is neither a neutral place of transient appetites or desires (the appetitive will) nor an executive active power under the command of reason (the active will): on the third conception, the will has a *substance* of its own. In other words, the will is a *faculty* of the mind in its own right; it is a 'motivational organ' *sui generis*. Talk about the deep nature, the identity and the character of a per-son's will only makes sense on this substantial conception, according to which the will has 'inherent proclivities of its own' independent from appe-tite and reason. My hypothesis as regards the interpretation of Frankfurt's overall view of the nature and the structure of the will is that both the appe-titive will and the active will are first and foremost conceptions of the will in direct connection to the metaphysical problem of freedom and determinism as discussed by compatibilists and incompatibilists, whereas the substantial will is a much more *phenomenological-existential* conception of the will in its own right. It is remarkable that Frankfurt in his more recent work is not troubled anymore about how what he says fits in the framework of compat-iblism and naturalism. What he offers of late is not so much an analytical metaphysics as an analytical *anthropology*. In what follows, I shall try to shed some light on the nature and the importance of the most substantial aspect of our volitional life.

As I understand Frankfurt's complex theory of the will, the substance of the 'motivational organ' of a person is shaped and configured by his *caring about, loving* and *being committed to* certain things. Examples of such inher-ent proclivities of the will include Luther's caring about a religious ideal as expressed by his declaring 'Here I stand; I can do no other', a mother's love for her child or a patriot's love for his country, and a person's commitment to one or another (moral) ideal such as the cause of justice. Now volitional dynamisms like these exhibit a special kind of necessity. Someone who cares about something is in general subject to what Frankfurt calls *volitional neces-sity*, i.e., 'a familiar but nonetheless somewhat obscure kind of necessity, in virtue of which his caring is not altogether under his own control' (Frankfurt, 1982, p. 86). Also, loving something is constrained by this volitional necessity not only because it cannot be started at will, but also because it remains for the most part outside direct and immediate voluntary control once started. Though the person is in no way logically or causally necessitated to act in accordance with his care or love, he cannot bring himself to alter his will and act otherwise. He simply is unwilling to counteract the constraining force and to opt for an alternative course of action. Yet the fact that he cannot do otherwise is neither due to a defect of his power to act nor to the lack of opportunity, but to a perplexity of his will.

Corresponding observations can be made with regard to the counterpart of volitional necessity, namely *unthinkability* (Frankfurt, 1988a, pp. 181-184). In a case of volitional necessity, a person can do no other than *A*; he is then unable to refrain from doing *A*. For example, the loving mother who cannot but run into the burning house to save her child at the risk of losing her own life. Conversely, in a case of unthinkability, a person cannot do *A*; he is then unable to perform *A* — doing *A* might just be unthinkable for him. For example, a well-trained soldier might nevertheless be unable to shoot innocent enemies in cold blood because such an action is too repugnant for him. Or, to take another example, a man of honour might be unable to follow an infamous course of conduct to save his life. Again, the fact that a person cannot do something which is unthinkable for him stems not from a logical or causal impossibility but from a perplexity of his volitional nature. Unthinkability, like volitional necessity, is a mode of necessity which sets limits to a person's will and thereby shapes the boundaries of his volitional identity. Now in as much as such necessities are outside a person's immediate and direct voluntary control and immune to deliberate change, they determine the invariable, permanent and stable volitional nature of that person. In other words, the necessities of the will — i.e., care, love and commitment as constrained by volitional necessity and unthinkability — constitute the *essence* of the will (Frankfurt, 1993, pp. 112-114).

Obviously, the necessities of the will resemble, in certain respects, overpowering compulsions and overwhelming aversions. A person is driven by internal forces or he runs up against internal obstacles which are not under his direct and immediate control, not only when he is subjected to volitional necessity in his care or love, but also when he is motivated by propelling passions or restraining feelings in his actions. However, whereas in the latter case we have passive happenings and therefore symptoms of heteronomy, in the former case we have activating processes which are conducive to *autonomy*. This last fact can, at least phenomenologically, be verified. A person whose behaviour is constrained by the necessities of his will does not, in general, experience his will as weakened or his freedom as diminished in any way. On the contrary, he feels himself volitionally strengthened and liberated in a special way. Even though his behaviour is not wholly under his direct and immediate volitional control, he feels more actively connected to his life. So the necessities of a person's will, paradoxically perhaps, seem to establish the autonomy of his will and to direct him towards his self-realization and self-fulfilment. How can this be?

Some of a person's 'irresistible inclinations' and 'insurmountable inhibitions' are not external to himself because he actively *identifies himself* with them. The fact that the necessities of a person's will are imposed by his own will partly accounts for the difference between the autonomy of volitional necessities and the heteronomy of compulsions and aversions which are involuntarily imposed by an alien force. However, although this self-imposition of volitional necessities undoubtedly is a condition for the autonomy of loving (or caring about) something, the more important condition for this autonomy resides in *the necessitating force of the loved object itself.* Volitional necessity is a genuine kind of necessity and, consequently, to keep its necessitating force, it cannot be voluntarily self-imposed alone but must, first and foremost, be involuntarily imposed by the loved object.

In light of the fact that the volitional necessity of loving is *both* voluntarily self-imposed *and* involuntarily imposed by the loved object, it might be helpful to compare the somewhat paradoxical phenomenon of loving as restricted by volitional necessity to the equally complex phenomenon of 'reverence for the law' that Immanuel Kant describes:

> Reverence is properly awareness of a value which demolishes my self-love. Hence there is something which is regarded neither as an object of inclination nor as an object of fear, though it has at the same time some analogy with both. The *object* of reverence is the *law* alone — the law which we impose *on ourselves* but yet as necessary in itself. Considered as a law, we are subject to it without any consultation of self-love; considered as self-imposed it is a consequence of our will. In the first respect it is analogous to fear, in the second to inclination. (Kant, 1785, p. 69)

When the obvious difference between Kant's impersonal moral law and Frankfurt's personal loved (or cared-about) object is put aside,[12] the comparison goes like this. Really, selflessly loving something is properly awareness of a value (of what is important) which demolishes my self-love. Hence, lov-

---

12. Frankfurt (1994) himself structurally compares the authority of love with that of Kantian duty.

ing something is neither just a matter of wanting or liking it nor a matter of being forced or coerced by it, 'though it has at the same time some analogy with both'. The *object* of real selfless love is the necessitating loved object alone — the necessitating force of the loved object (the volitional necessity) which the person voluntarily imposes on himself 'but yet as necessary in itself', i.e., as a necessitating object in itself it also imposes itself involuntarily. Considered as imposed involuntarily, the person is subject to it without any consultation of his self-love or self-interest; considered as self-imposed it is a consequence of his will or self-identification. In the first respect it is analogous to coercion, in the second to liking. So a loving person who is constrained by volitional necessity, like one revering the moral law, is at the same time both active (voluntary) and passive (involuntary) with regard to the same force.

Volitional necessity as a genuine kind of *necessity* must be involuntarily imposed by the loved (or cared-about) object. Regardless of whether the person likes it or not, the loved object imposes necessities upon his will and maintains its constraints. Because of this involuntary imposition, the person subjected to the volitional necessity of his love is, so to speak, *captivated* by the object he loves. His selfless and necessitated dedication to the loved object makes him in a way a *prisoner* of that object. However, as suggested above, this captivation or imprisonment by 'irresistible inclinations' and 'insurmountable inhibitions' does not enslave him but, on the contrary, it sets him free and enhances his autonomy. Now it is not difficult to understand why the self-imposition of such necessities can have a liberating effect since the self-identifying 'deep self' of the hierarchical model is here once again the source of autonomy. Yet, whatever the liberating impact of active self-imposition may be, how can the *passivity* of volitional necessity as such be conducive to *autonomy*? How can it be understood that the necessitating force of the loved object itself has a liberating effect? Why does love in itself set free?

In order to see why autonomy intrinsically comprises volitional necessity, let us start from the opposite situation in which a person is not at all under the spell of some loved object. Without the guidance of one or other loved object, a person is 'the slave of his passions'. His desires and emotions come and go, following no determinate pattern. The anarchy of his capricious desires will be disruptive for him and drive him to distraction; although he can act as he pleases. Owing to the lack of fixed goals and unified purposes, his motivational and emotional life is utterly chaotic. Despite the fact that his natural conative energies are unchained, this person might well find his life shallow and without any point as he suffers from 'the unbearable lightness of being'. However, when such a person starts loving a certain object, he becomes identified with it and subjected to its necessitating force. By falling under the spell of the loved object, he begins to guide his motivational and emotional life in the light of it. By virtue of its necessitating impact, the loved object provides the person with a unity of purpose and a stable goal in view of which he can integrate his desires and passions. Anarchic liberty, emotional chaos and distraction are thereby replaced by unity as well as stability of purpose and *authentic freedom*. By providing guidance, the loved object liberates the person *from* his natural inner chaos and makes him free *for* the pursuit of what he truly loves. The necessitating force of the loved object disconnects the person from the arbitrariness of his 'bundle of desires' and actively connects him to what most truly realizes and fulfils himself. So even though the necessitating force of the loved object imposes itself involuntary, such a volitional necessity may have a distinctively *liberating* effect: 'It is in this way that volitional necessity may have a liberating effect: when someone is tending to be distracted from caring about what he cares about most, the force of volitional necessity may constrain him to do what he really wants to do.' (Frankfurt, 1982, p. 88) Volitional necessity thus provides for liberty and invigorates life. Consequently, self-realization, self-fulfilment and autonomy in an authentic sense are not opposed to volitional necessity but *positively require* it.

The doctrine of volitional foundationalism

Thus far I made a tripartite distinction between conceptions of the will — as appetitive, active and substantial — to make sense of Frankfurt's overall view of the nature and the structure of the will. Now Frankfurt's theory of the will is not only complex but also *layered*. The three conceptions of the will are not merely distinct: the one type of willing also depends upon the other for its proper functioning. Although epistemological foundationalism may be on the wane, Frankfurt innovatively develops his complex theory of the will into a form of what I call *volitional foundationalism*. This doctrine holds that willing as caring about or loving something as restricted by volitional necessity constitutes the foundation upon which the organization of a person's will and the execution of his acts of will rest. Accordingly, the substantial will is the volitional bedrock in which the active and the appetitive will are founded. Frankfurt establishes his volitional foundationalism in the context of what I label a 'hybrid' theory of personal autonomy and an attendant 'asymmetrical dependency' thesis concerning self-identification (Cuypers, 2000). Explicating the reason why the substantial will is foundational and how it plays a pivotal role in Frankfurt's theory of autonomy is my next task. Let me start by characterizing the latter theory in light of what went before.

Once his theory of the will is in place, it is not difficult to appreciate that Frankfurt's accompanying theory of personal autonomy is *hybrid*. To my mind, two major conceptions of autonomy are at work in Frankfurt's analytical anthropology. On the one hand, autonomy is constituted by choosing, decision-making and, consequently, by *decisive self-identification*. According to this first conception, autonomy depends upon the active will — autonomous choices and decisions stand wholly under a person's voluntary control. This *voluntaristic* conception, as I call it, aligns with the standard definition of autonomy: 'An autonomous agent is, by definition, governed by himself alone. He acts entirely under his own control.' (Frankfurt, 1994, p. 132) On the other hand, autonomy is constituted by *caring* (or loving) as constrained by volitional necessity. According to this second conception, autonomy depends upon the substantial will — due to the necessities of the will caring and loving are, to a considerable extent, beyond a person's immediate voluntary control. This *non-voluntaristic* conception, as I call it, is non-standard: 'A person acts autonomously only when his volitions derive from the essential character of his will.' (Frankfurt, 1994, p. 132) Some volitions which derive from the essential character of a person's will are not under his immediate voluntary control because they are constrainted by volitional necessity. In as much as the constitution of a person's volitional identity is beyond and outside his direct and immediate voluntary control, he is, to that extent, not of his own making but the product of destiny.

It is clear, I think, that two distinct conceptions of autonomy are present in Frankfurt's model. My foregoing sketch provides sufficient evidence to support my claim that the concept of autonomy is hybrid. However, the concept of autonomy does not just comprise two distinct and otherwise unrelated conceptions of autonomy. Rather, the conceptions are related in the following way. The voluntaristic conception of autonomy as decision-making *asymmetrically* depends upon the non-voluntaristic conception of autonomy as caring.[13] That is to say, voluntarism depends upon non-voluntarism, but not vice versa since the dependency relation is asymmetrical. The dependency only goes one way, namely from decision-making to caring. Let me first state this asymmetrical dependency thesis more clearly and then give an argument for it, which also establishes the doctrine of volitional foundationalism as a corollary.

Since autonomy is constituted by self-identification in Frankfurt's hierar-

---

13. I borrow the term 'asymmetrical dependency' from Jerry Fodor (1990, pp. 91-95) who uses it, in an altogether different context, while explaining his informational (psycho)semantics.

chical model of autonomy, the asymmetrical dependency thesis can, I propose, most perspicuously be stated in terms of (self-)identification. It says:

> Genuine and effective identification (with desires) through forming decisive second-order volitions asymmetrically depends upon identification (with desires) through caring about something as restricted by volitional necessity.

As stated by this thesis, identification through caring about something as restricticted by volitional necessity is basic. But what exactly does this type of identification mean? The process of caring about something is in an important way tantamount to a process of identification. This is so because caring about something means, so to speak, being invested in that thing with one's own personality. It means being dedicated or devoted to that thing with one's heart and soul. If a person cares, for example, about his own personal projects and ideals or loves certain individuals and groups, then he *is identified* with those cared-about or loved objects in the sense that *he himself* becomes susceptible to their good and bad fortunes. When his cared-about or loved objects are affected positively or negatively, he himself is affected accordingly. If one of a person's ideals is betrayed, he himself is betrayed; if a member of his family is honoured, he himself is honoured. Because of the relationship between himself and his cared-about or loved objects, his own personal fate is intimately bound up with the fate of those objects. Moreover, since caring about something is restricted by volitional necessity, the things a person cares about are expressive of his *substantial volitional identity.* The basic mechanism for building and maintaining the *authentic and deep nature* of the will resides in caring about something as restricted by volitional necessity. The volitional necessities to which he is subjected delineate the fixed form of his volitional identity; they constitute the essence of his will. And in view of the fact that a person essentially is a volitional entity, a person's essential identity coincides with his will's essence:

> The essence of a person, ..., is a matter of the contingent volitional necessities by which the will of the person is as a matter of fact constrained. ... They are substantive rather than merely formal. They pertain to the purposes, the preferences, and the other characteristics that the individual cannot help having and that effectively determine the activities of his will. (Frankfurt, 1994, p. 138)

So the necessities of the will constitute the will's essence, and what pertains

126

to a person's volitional essence is intrinsically internal to the identity of that person. In this sense, a person not only identifies with the things he cares about, he also *is* those things.

Let us now take a closer look at the asymmetrical dependency thesis. In the present context, the relation of asymmetrical dependency is best construed as a relation among identifications. Identifications themselves are intentional and/or causal relations. The (second-order) relation of asymmetrical dependency can then be expressed in terms of subjunctive conditionals (counterfactuals): if there were no (or had not been) identifications through caring, then there would not be (or would not have been) genuine and effective identifications through decision-making, but not the other way around. There being genuine and effective identifications through caring does not depend upon there being identifications through decision-making. That is, what prevents identifications through decision-making from being self-deceptive, akratic and powerless is that they are restricted and informed by identifications through caring. In virtue of its volitional necessity non-voluntaristic identification establishes the necessary constraints and tendencies to make voluntaristic identification *wholehearted*.

The asymmetrical dependency thesis implies that self-identification through caring must be the *original* source of autonomy whereas decisive self-identification can only be the *derivative* source. The non-voluntaristic conception of autonomy as constituted by self-identification throught caring about something is *primary* while the voluntaristic conception of autonomy as constituted by decisive self-identification is only *secondary*.[14] Now because the relationship between voluntaristic or active identification and non-voluntaristic or passive identification is one of asymmetrical dependency, the thesis implies further that the non-voluntaristic conception of autonomy is more fundamental than the voluntaristic one. As a result, caring about something as restricted by volitional necessity constitutes the *ultimate foundation* upon which the organization of a person's will and the execution of his acts of will rest. In other words, the asymmetrical dependency thesis has as a consequence the doctrine of volitional foundationalism. This foundationalism follows from the fact that the dependency only goes one way. The

---

14. Whereas an identification through forming a decisive second-order volition is an event that is fairly limited in time, an identification through caring about something is *a process that takes a considerable amount of time*. That is to say, the latter type of identification is a *historical* phenomenon. So in spite of the fact that voluntaristic autonomy is, according to Frankfurt, just a matter of taking a decisive attitude at a certain moment (time-slice) and, consequently, that voluntaristic autonomy is *not* a historical phenomenon, the ultimate non-voluntaristic foundations of voluntaristic autonomy clearly are historical. Though I will not pursue the matter here, this historical dimension in Frankfurt's hybrid theory of autonomy seems to be relevant for Fischer's and Ravizza's (1994) important discussion of Frankfurt's hierarchical model.

active (as well as the appetitive) will, for its authentic autonomy, thus asymmetrically depends upon the basic substantial will, but not vice versa. To be sure, this doctrine of volitional foundationalism goes against the grain of dominant contemporary analytical thinking about the nature of the will and the constitution of personal autonomy. The conception of the active will — as well as of the appetitive will which for the solution of the regress problem depends upon the active one — and the concomitant conception of voluntaristic autonomy are the only ones standardly analyzed in the analytical debate. Let me now then offer an argument to show that this neglect of the substantial will and non-voluntaristic autonomy is a serious mistake.

We tend to think that the hard core of personal autonomy resides in the limitless and boundless activity of the active will. That is to say, we commonly assume that the unlimited expansion of opportunity and the unbounded enlargement of freedom of choice and decision are always instrumental to the development of autonomy and the realization of the ideal of individuality. We uncritically take it for granted that the more unlimited and unbounded we become, the more autonomous and self-realized we will be. This widespread thought rests, however, on an important existential mistake (Frankfurt, 1993, pp. 109-110). Personal autonomy and self-identity cannot indefinitely be enhanced and enriched by a further and further proliferation of options and possibilities of choice and decision. This is so because too much opportunity and too many alternatives to choose from corrode a person's self-confidence, paralyze his capacity for effective decision-making and in the end cause him to be completely indifferent in view of the infinite range of options and choices. In other words, too much unrestricted liberty destroys a person's capacity for practical reasoning and makes him irrational or, even worse, insane. With no limits to freedom anything goes, even monstrous possibilities would then become thinkable options.

Furthermore, and more thoroughly, if the boundaries of a person's will were *themselves* among the range of his options to choose from or to decide upon, then his will would lose all 'substance' — that is, fixed background — needed to guide his acts of will. What could guide a person in choosing and deciding if the principles of choice and decision are among the very things that he must choose from and decide upon? Without an antecedently fixed volitional identity, a person lacks an authentic and authoritative basis for choice and decision — the acts of will simply go mad (Frankfurt, 1988a, pp. 177-178). Consequently, personal autonomy and self-identity *require boundaries and restrictions fixed in advance.* We must be bounded to be free. Now these boundaries are luckily set by the necessities of the will. In virtue of its volitional necessity (or unthinkability), caring about (or loving or being

128

committed to) something establishes the necessary restrictions within which practical reasoning can operate in a rational and sane way. The genuine autonomy of the active will, therefore, depends upon the authentic autonomy of the substantial will.

Of course, this argument for the asymmetrical dependency thesis also establishes the doctrine of volitional foundationalism as a corollary. Let me spell it out. As the argument shows, the basic mode of practical rationality resides in the substantial will. The substantial will binds and limits itself, so to speak, by volitional necessity or unthinkability in order to keep its mental sanity and to preserve itself. Due to its self-binding and self-limitation, the *inherent* rationality of the substantial will does not derive from the independent faculty of reason or from the active will under the command of reason. As the above argument further shows, the active will — choice-making or decision-taking — depends, for its rationality and sanity, upon the substantial will. And in its turn, the appetitive will (second-order volition), for the solution of the regress problem, depends upon the active will. Consequently, the substantial will is the *ultimate foundation* of our volitional and practical rational capacities.

The doctrine of volitional foundationalism — the combination of a hybrid thesis about the concept of personal autonomy with an attendant asymmetrical dependency thesis regarding self-identification — justifies, I submit, the first part of my moderately heteronomous view of personal autonomy, namely passive self-identification. It directly follows from this doctrine that the process of self-identification cannot entirely be rooted in autonomous acts of the will such as decision and choice. As stated by the asymmetrical dependency thesis, the process of self-identification is first and foremost rooted in the *passive* processes of caring about (or loving or being committed to) something as constrained by volitional necessity. In addition, Frankfurt's adherence to the doctrine of volitional foundationalism — especially to the hybrid thesis — makes sense of his equivocal employment of the concept of the will and explains the perhaps surprising fact that his theory of personal autonomy is not only partly in line with the extremely autonomous view but also partly in accord with my moderately heteronomous view.

Chapter Six

Community and Authenticity of the Self

Introduction

My moderately heteronomous view of personal identity is based on two claims: firstly, that the process of self-identification cannot entirely be rooted in autonomous acts of the will such as decision and choice, and secondly, that the process of self-evaluation depends in an important sense on the normative impact of other people's attitudes. In this final chapter, I will develop further the second half of my moderately heteronomous view, namely social self-evaluation. For that purpose, I shall construct a community view of personal identity — culminating in an elucidation of the self's authenticity — by using some key ideas of Wittgenstein as they can be found in his later writings. So my objective here is the understanding of the nature and the importance of personal autonomy within a broadly Wittgensteinian framework for the sake of deepening my own position.

In the *Philosophical Investigations* Wittgenstein (1953, I, § 122) writes:

> ... A perspicuous representation produces just that understanding which consists in 'seeing connexions'. ... The concept of a perspicuous representation is of fundamental significance to us. It earmarks the form of account we give, the way we look at things. ...

As indicated in the introductory chapter, the positive task of analytical philosophy lies, along the lines of this quotation, in the construction of a perspicuous representation (*übersichtliche Darstellung*). Hopefully, 'nothing is hidden' in the final analysis, yet in the beginning everything lacks perspicuity. Although Wittgenstein himself never developed a perspicuous representation of personal autonomy and authenticity in his own writings, I shall in this chapter construct such a representation. My construction of a Wittgensteinian outlook on this existential and moral theme is based on Harry Frankfurt's hierarchical model of the self and Charles Taylor's moral psychology. My main conclusion of this applied Wittgensteinian philosophy — of a community view — is that the true nature of autonomy cannot be radi-

131

cal self-determination but must be authenticity, which involves as possibility conditions the recognition by other people (social dependence) as well as horizons of significance (forms of life). As a final point, I will investigate the importance of the ideal of authenticity in the moral and political context of feminism and communitarianism.

A Wittgensteinian outlook on personal autonomy

At first glance, it might seem that Wittgenstein cannot be of any help to understand the nature and the importance of personal autonomy. Nowhere in his works can one find a perspicuous representation of this theme. Although Wittgenstein briefly remarked upon the issues of the subject and the person, especially in the context of solipsism (Wittgenstein, 1922, 5.63-5.64; 1958, pp. 61-74), he never even tried to see the connections between the concept of personal autonomy and other clarifying concepts such as that of decision-making or that of the will in general. Wittgenstein never elaborated an analytical anthropology (as I understand it here) and thus never explored the role of personal autonomy or that of authenticity in human life. Of course, this is not at all surprising, since Wittgenstein invested the bulk of his philosophical energy in semantical and epistemological (and to a lesser extent, ontological) topics. One can therefore wonder what, if anything, Wittgenstein has to say about the way we look at personal autonomy.

Notwithstanding the fact that Wittgenstein never explicitly dealt with analytical anthropology, I suggest that Wittgenstein's pure philosophical views can have illuminating implications for such an anthropology. To my mind, the application of his semantical and epistemological views to issues in analytical anthropology such as self-identity and personal autonomy can readily provide a counterbalance to theoretical accounts which are too mentalistic and too individualistic in the interpretation they give of these issues. If one takes my suggestion seriously, it is to be expected that what Wittgenstein has to say in philosophy in general will be equally fruitful when applied to other less semantical or epistemological and more existential or moral concepts, among which the concept of personal autonomy. The fact that these concepts are less 'theoretical' and more 'practical' does not exclude in advance the possibility of an applied Wittgensteinian philosophy. Thus, while one cannot reconstruct in any direct way Wittgenstein's view of existential or moral topics, one can try to construct a Wittgensteinian outlook on such topics as personal autonomy. That is at least what I shall try to do in this chapter. My perspicuous representation will then offer not so much what Wittgenstein actually said as what he *would have* said about the nature and the importance of personal autonomy.

But even granted the possibility of an applied Wittgensteinian philosophy, the application of Wittgenstein's pure philosophy to the topic at issue might still seem at first sight unfruitful and even impossible. Indeed, an analysis of the concept of personal autonomy seems blatantly incompatible with the currently predominant interpretation of Wittgenstein's later philosophy, the philosophy consolidated in the *Investigations* (1953). This interpretation has come to be known as the *community view* (Kripke, 1984). In this view the Cartesian privilege of the first person is radically abolished, while the primacy of the third person is firmly installed in its place, especially in connection with semantics. The individual person, considered in isolation, lacks the capacity to constitute meaning and rule-following. Instead, it is argued that social agreement in *form of life* and social customs (uses, institutions) are *necessary* for the very possibility of meaning and rule-following (Wittgenstein, 1953, I, § 241; 199). Consequently, if applying Wittgenstein's pure philosophy comes to the same thing as applying the community view, then a Wittgensteinian outlook on personal autonomy does not seem feasible at first sight. This is so because it is commonly thought that social interference in whatever way poses a serious threat to personal autonomy. According to this widespread view, 'autonomy' and 'community' are mutually exclusive terms in the sense that the creativity of the autonomous individual is thought to be suffocated by the conformism of the community. How can a person be called autonomous if what he is and does necessarily depends upon the judgements of other people? How can he earn the title of autonomous being if his identity is radically moulded under the influence of the social environment?

However, I shall try to show that Wittgenstein's general picture as outlined by the community view of the *Investigations* is only at variance with a narcissistic and corrupt conception of personal autonomy. This conception has to be considered as a deviant form of the more moral and ideal conception of personal autonomy as *authenticity*. The moral ideal of authenticity is not at all in opposition to the community view of the human condition. Quite on the contrary, true personal autonomy *presupposes* the impact of other people's attitudes and the larger communal context. Thus, although social dependence is usually regarded as incompatible with personal autonomy, this dependence on other people's opinions and social frameworks is not so much an impediment as it is a *constitutive* contribution to authentic autonomy.

For this reason, a Wittgensteinian outlook on personal autonomy seems possible after all. To develop this theme I have, surprisingly perhaps, no need to start from scratch. My construction of this outlook as well as its defence is based upon two major views in contemporary philosophical anthropology, namely Frankfurt's hierarchical model of the self and Taylor's moral psychology. In an important sense, which will hopefully become clear during my construction, what Wittgenstein *would have said* about personal autonomy is to a large extent the same as what Frankfurt and Taylor *actually say* about it.

The use of 'I' as subject and the hierarchical model

Although Wittgenstein in the later period of his life possibly changed, or at least relaxed, his views on solipsism, he never changed his views on the self or the subject. From beginning to end, his analytical anthropology remained through and through *anti-Cartesian*. Thus, in the *Tractatus Logico-Philosophicus* Wittgenstein (1922, 5.631) states:

> The thinking, presenting subject; there is no such thing. If I wrote a book 'The world as I found it', I should also have therein to report on my body and say which members obey my will and which do not, etc. This then would be a method of isolating the subject or rather of showing that in an important sense there is no subject: that is to say, of it alone in this book mention could *not* be made.

And again, near the end of *The Blue Book* (1958, p. 69) he writes:

> We feel then that in the cases in which 'I' is used as subject, we don't use it because we recognize a particular person by his bodily characteristics; and this creates the illusion that we use this word to refer to something bodiless, which, however, has its seat in our body. In fact *this* seems to be the real ego, the one of which it was said, 'Cogito, ergo sum'.

Parfit (1984, p. 273) claims that Wittgenstein's rejection of the Cartesian ego theory directly implies that Wittgenstein *would have* agreed with the empiricist bundle theory of self-identity. Facing a choice between two views of a person's self-identity, Wittgenstein would have rejected the metaphysical view that the self-identity of a person involves the identity of his soul-substance and, consequently, he would have accepted the alternative empiricist view that a person's self-identity consists in the continuity of the bundle of his experiences. However, Wittgenstein's anti-Cartesianism does not in and of itself implicate empiricism with regard to the constitution of the self. Wittgenstein (1958, p. 66) clearly distinguishes between two different uses of the word 'I': its use as subject and its use as object. Most importantly, 'I' in its use as subject is irreducible to 'I' in its use as object, in which case it refers to the person's body (Wittgenstein, 1958, p. 74). Now, as Thomas Nagel (1986, pp. 32-37; 54-66) convincingly argued, if the first-person pronoun is used to refer to the bundle of experiences, then 'I' cannot be used as subject, but only as object. To adapt Wittgenstein's first sentence of the passage from *The Blue Book* quoted above: In the cases in which 'I' is used as subject, we equally don't use it because we recognize a particular person by his *psychological* characteristics. The bundle of experiences belongs as much to the objective world as the person's body. The psychological I would certainly be mentioned in the book 'The world as I found it'. But, of course, because we do use 'I' *as subject*:

> There is [therefore] really a sense in which in philosophy we can talk of a non-psychological I. ... The philosophical I is not the man, not the human body or the human soul of which psychology treats, but the metaphysical subject, the limit — not a part of the world. (Wittgenstein, 1922, 5.641)

Wittgenstein's notion of 'the metaphysical subject' raises difficult semantical and ontological questions about self-reference and self-constitution. In my attempt to apply Wittgenstein's pure philosophy to more existential and moral issues, these intricate problems can luckily be set aside. Suffice it to say that the metaphysical subject is neither a soul-substance nor a bundle of experiences: it's a non-Cartesian as well as a non-psychological self. A Wittgensteinian outlook on personal autonomy must then at least be compatible with this negative ontology of the self. Positively we can say, I think, that when we talk in philosophy about the metaphysical subject as the limit of the world we are talking, as Nagel (1986, p. 62, n. 3) claims, about *subjectivity*. Although 'I' in its use as subject does not refer to a special entity which has its seat in a person's body, it still expresses or indicates the subjectivity of a person. The fact that in an important sense there are no such *things* as subjects does not preclude the fact that in another equally important sense there really exist centres of subjectivity. *Pace* Norman Malcolm (1988), to admit the existence of subjectivity in the world does not amount to the same thing as endorsing Cartesianism again.

The best model to represent the essential subjectivity of the person is, I think, the hierarchical model of the self and its autonomy, as set out by Frankfurt. Since I have given particulars of the model before, I only will highlight the main points again. This model comprises two major elements. Firstly, since subjectivity always involves self-consciousness, and since the structure which 'I' in its use as subject expresses necessarily entails reflexivity, we can draw a hierarchical distinction between mental states (events, processes) of the *first order* and those of the *second* or *higher order*. And secondly: taking into consideration my endeavour to render Wittgenstein's pure philosophy useful for the existential and moral domains, we are not so much interested in the 'theoretical' part of the mind as in its 'practical' part. A person's essential subjectivity is therefore more germane to his *will* than to his reason; the existential essence of a person has more to do with his *volitions* or *desires* than with his beliefs. If we are interested in the moral dimension and the meaning of a person's life, we are particularly concerned with the structure of his motives and the pattern of his actions which flows from that motivational structure. Consequently, taking the two elements together, we can say that the hierarchical model of the self represents the essential subjectivity of the person in that it concentrates on his motivational structure which is composed of first-order and second-order desires and volitions. As an example of such a complex volitional structure, consider a corpulent weightwatcher who not only desires to be slim, but also does not desire that (s)he desires to eat sweets.

In terms of this model's central notion of a hierarchy of desires and volitions, different central notions in analytical anthropology can fruitfully be analyzed. Among these anthropological notions the most salient are autonomy, self-identification, self-evaluation, authenticity, self-constitution, ego-ideal, self-change, internal conflict, self-fulfilment and weakness of the will. Here I will only draw attention to the autonomy of the self and self-evaluation.

When a person cares about himself, he cares about his will because his identity — what he really is — is particularly constituted by his volitional character. Out of a special self-love, a person normally is not indifferent to the structure of his will. This means that he takes an evaluative attitude towards his own volitions. It is this capacity for reflective *self-evaluation* that is manifested in the formation of second-order desires and volitions. When a person takes a pro-attitude towards a certain part of his own will, he forms a positive desire (or volition) of the second order with regard to a certain desire (or volition) of the first order. And conversely, when a person takes a contra-attitude, he forms a negative desire of the second order. Now in the event that a person forms a positive second-order desire with reference to a first-order desire, we can also say that he *identifies* himself with his will. And, if a person can reflectively identify himself with his desires of the first order, then he has a positively free will. In other words, when there exists a conformity of a person's first-order desires to his second-order desires, he enjoys *autonomy*. He determines himself, if he has a will he wants to have.

But if he has a will he does not want to have, he is estranged from himself. To put it succinctly, autonomy is volitional harmony. Or, to keep faith with the etymology of the term, auto-nomy is self-rule: a person rules himself by evaluating his desires of the lower order according to his own desires of the higher order. This self-evaluation amounts to 'self-government': the government of a person by the person himself.

Admittedly, the hierarchical model of the use of 'I' as subject is certainly not a standard Wittgensteinian picture. Although it models the reflexive will which is the seat of existential or moral significance, it is still much too psychological: 'Of the will as the subject of the ethical we cannot speak. And the will as a phenomenon is only of interest to psychology.' (Wittgenstein, 1922, 6.423) Nonetheless, the suggested model is, I think, at least compatible with the use of 'I' as subject, especially in a less semantical or epistemological context. Moreover, this model does not presuppose the picture theory of meaning which undeniably informs the quoted passage from the *Tractatus*, but it rather invites the view that meaning is use. Be that as it may, in order to interpret other more existential remarks of Wittgenstein, the hierarchical model seems right on the mark: '*Nobody can truthfully say of himself that he is filth*. Because if I do say it, though it can be true in a sense, this is not a truth by which I myself can be penetrated: otherwise I should either have to go mad or change myself.' (Wittgenstein, 1980, p. 32e) In this passage quoted from *Culture and Value* Wittgenstein is surely commenting on self-evaluation, (the lack of) autonomy and self-change in a much more psychological setting and against an existential or moral background.

Apart from the problem of a possible infinite regress, the most notoriously troublesome aspect of the hierarchical model of the self and its autonomy is, as pointed out before, the problem of *normativity*. The difficulty which pertains to the authority which second-order desires (or volitions) apparently have in the hierarchical model of self-evaluation is the following. By taking pro-attitudes or contra-attitudes of the second order towards his desires of the first order, a person evaluates his volitional system. But were do these evaluative attitudes get their authoritative or normative power from? On the hierarchical account, second-order attitudes are, after all, just like the first-order desires they evaluate, *simply desires*. Going up one level does not automatically confer an evaluative authority upon desires of the second order; desires, of whatever order, can never have, of themselves, a special normative status. The difficulty here is not so much that there is a possibility of a regressive ascent, but rather that nothing about the level of desires gives them any special authority with respect to self-evaluation. Watson (1975) has sharply pointed out this difficulty and, in order to overcome it, he has recommended a distinction between desiring and *valuing*, between a volitional and a *valuation system*. To have an evaluative authority, higher-order attitudes — second-order desires and volitions — must be grounded in the values of the person which themselves cannot simply be reduced to his desires. Thus, the question of normativity boils down to the question as to what *constitutes* a person's valuation system.

The community view of meaning as significance

It is to this important question of normativity, I think, that a distinctively Wittgensteinian answer can be suggested. To be sure, no straightforward answer of Wittgenstein, or even a broadly Wittgensteinian answer, is readily available. My construction of a Wittgensteinian outlook on the normativity of self-evaluation starts from a rough analogy between meaning *as sense (and reference)* on the one hand and meaning *as significance (or value)* on the other hand. Meaning as significance is partly analogous to meaning as sense. A Wittgensteinian picture of autonomy only manifests itself when Wittgenstein's semantical views on meaning in language are applied to *existential* meaning or 'the meaning of life'. Again, the distinction between the two modes of meaning(fulness) I have in mind is that between meaning as external referential or semantic relation on the one hand and meaning as personal significance, relevance, importance, value, mattering on the other (Nozick, 1981, p. 574). Roughly speaking, philosophers of language and logic — and so Wittgenstein himself — concentrate on semantic meaning, while philosophers of man and morals attend to personal meaning. When we talk about the meaning of linguistic entities such as the word 'cow' and the sentence 'The cat is on the mat', the first mode of meaning is under consideration. Yet when we say, for example, 'She means a lot to him' or 'The principle of equality means a lot to socialists', the second mode of meaning is at issue. Of course, it is this second mode of meaning(fulness) — meaning as value — that is at stake in the problems of autonomy and self-evaluation. A person who says of himself that 'he is filth' and, consequently, whose volitional structure is not indifferent to him, cares about the meaning or value of his life.

The question as to what constitutes a person's valuation system or, generally speaking, meaning as value can now be treated analogously to the question as to what constitutes meaning as sense. To this latter semantic question it is very plausible, as I mentioned at the outset of this chapter, to give the answer of the so-called *community view*. According to this view's interpretation of Wittgenstein's *anti-private language argument*, the normativity of meaning as sense cannot be accounted for unless the authority of the linguistic community is invoked. In a nutshell, the line of argumentation

138

goes like this. The concept of semantic meaning is normative: 'The relation of meaning and intention to future action is *normative*, not *descriptive*.' (Kripke, 1984, p. 37) However, a single person considered in isolation is utterly incapable to constitute normative meaning: 'In particular, this point applies if I direct my attention to a sensation and name it: nothing I have done determines future applications (in the sense of being uniquely *justified* by the concept grasped).' (Kripke, 1984, p. 107) Therefore, the normative concept of meaning is social: '... if the individual in question no longer conforms to what the community would do in these circumstances, the community can no longer attribute the concept to him.' (Kripke, 1984, p. 95)

Now if there is something to gain from the analogy between meaning as sense and meaning as significance, then a distinctively Wittgensteinian answer can be suggested to the initial existential question as to what constitutes a person's valuation system. This answer, surprisingly perhaps, can be found in Charles Taylor's work on the nature of the moral self. Although he himself only rarely brings out his allegiance to a broadly Wittgensteinian framework (but see Taylor, 1989, pp. 35; 38), Taylor implicitly but clearly develops a community view of *personal* meaning, and even gives an anti-private *significance* argument in support of this view. It is to Taylor's central ideas about the issues of autonomy and self-evaluation — ideas which have, to my mind, a recognizable Wittgensteinian flavour — that I now turn. In my construction of this Wittgensteinian outlook on personal autonomy, I will focus on Taylor's minor study *The Ethics of Authenticity* (1991) instead of on his major study *The Sources of the Self* (1989) because the former recapitulates the basic view and the main arguments of the latter in a more formal as well as more accessible way.

Modernity and the need for recognition by other people

Confronted with the problem of normativity, the modern Western, liberal, educated and secular person unhesitatingly opts for the currently obvious solution. The straightforward answer to the question as to what constitutes a person's valuation system is, needless to say, that the person himself determines his own values. This *self-determination of values* directly flows from moral subjectivism and soft relativism both of which are offshoots of radical individualism, the hallmark of modernity. To say that the modern person is the 'self-determining autonomous person' has become a tautology:

> ... everyone has a right to develop their own form of life, grounded on their own sense of what is really important or of value. People are called upon to be true to themselves and to

seek their own self-fulfilment. What this consists of, each must, in the last instance, determine for him- or herself. No one else can or should try to dictate its content. (Taylor, 1991, p. 14)

The valuation system of a modern person must, therefore, be grounded in a *radically free choice* or *decision of his own*. That is so because in his self-evaluation an autonomous person can neither submit himself to a pre-established religious or moral authority nor to any socially prevalent system of values and norms. He has the absolute right of self-creation as regards the manner as well as the matter (or content) of his life.

Unmistakably, this modern individualism of self-fulfilment collides head-on with a community view of personal meaning or value. However, the individualistic and even narcissistic conception of personal autonomy is, according to Taylor (1991, pp. 15-16), only a debased and travestied expression of a more adequate conception of being true to oneself. And this more moral and ideal conception of having one's own original way, for which he uses the phrase 'the ideal of *authenticity*', does incorporate a community view of the constitution of a person's valuation system. Not only is such a community view compatible with the ideal of authenticity, it is even a conceptual prerequisite of being in true contact with oneself. In short, atomistically isolated autonomy which radically excludes social interference is a deviant form of authenticity which only flourishes in a social context. In this way, Taylor's retrieval of the ideal of authenticity from our modern culture of narcissism and self-indulgence comes to the same thing as elaborating a community view of the nature and importance of the higher ideal behind the egoistic and hedonistic practices of people in the age of modernity.

As against the reactionaries who try to knock down all forms of individualism in contemporary society, the importance or worthiness of authenticity can be defended in terms of its essential relation to *the good life* and *human happiness*. Taking into consideration the human aspirations as such, the validity of authenticity as an ideal in human life is self-evident:

> ... in articulating this ideal [of authenticity] over the last two centuries, Western culture has identified one of the important potentialities of human life. Like other facets of modern individualism ... authenticity points us towards a more self-responsible form of life. It allows us to live (potentially) a fuller and more differentiated life, because more fully appropriated as our own. ... at its best authenticity allows a richer mode of existence. (Taylor, 1991, p. 74)

140

Indeed, the role of authenticity in the modern Western world is unquestionably constitutive of what it means to lead a distinctively human life. Brought into existence as much by the Enlightenment as by Romanticism, the ideal of authenticity is here to stay, for better or for worse. The pessimists who try to debunk all appeals to self-realization too readily forget that individualism does not in and of itself bring a loss of meaning and a fading of moral horizons — the 'disenchantment' of the world — in its wake. But, of course, they are right to point out the dangers of the subjectivist turn which the pursuit of self-fulfilment quite recently took.

As against the boosters of the contemporary culture of narcissism who happily embrace its liberating relativism and subjectivism, the self-defeating structure of radical autonomy or self-determining freedom can be convincingly demonstrated. Such a demonstration directly follows from an articulation of the nature of the ideal of authenticity in terms of a *community view* of personal meaning or significance. By way of rational argumentation, Taylor tries to show that the corrupt self-centred forms of being true to oneself are in the end narrow and shallow because these forms destroy the very possibility conditions of leading an authentic life. His overall argument consists of two mutually supporting parts: firstly, the more concrete considerations from *the need for recognition*, and secondly, the more abstract considerations from *horizons of significance*. It is these latter considerations which constitute, to my mind, an anti-private significance argument that runs parallel to Wittgenstein's famous anti-private language argument in semantics and epistemology. Before exposing this argument against private significance in the next section, I deal with the first possibility condition for truly authentic autonomy.

Taylor's general argument takes as its premiss our shared human condition and then tries to remind us of certain general features of human life in support of his argumentation (Taylor, 1991, pp. 32; 56). This procedure calls to mind a well-known methodological point of Wittgenstein:

> What we are supplying are really remarks on the natural history of human beings; we are not contributing curiosities however, but observations which no one has doubted, but which have escaped remark only because they are always before our eyes. (Wittgenstein, 1953, I, § 415)

One general fact about our shared human condition which Taylor tries to remind us of is that the definition of our identity essentially depends upon the recognition we get from what George Herbert Mead called *significant others*. (Taylor, 1991, p. 33) Persons are not like self-contained monads. The

141

existential identity of a person — his self-esteem — is not built in a mono-logical, but in a *dialogical* way. Through the medium of languages of expression, the exchange between the self and the other constitutes the *narrative* identity of the self (Taylor, 1989, pp. 35; 47). Of course, it is almost a commonplace to say that human beings are deeply involved with other human beings. However, the involvement with other people in the definition of our identity is not only a temporal genetical, but also an everlasting structural feature of our lives. Moreover, the reference to other people in the delineation of 'who we are' is not so much extrinsic and instrumental, as it is intrinsic and constitutive. Our dealings with other selves cannot be thought of on the model of a social contract between fundamentally isolated individuals. Quite the reverse is the case, for we are always already caught in an original social web of attitudes and reactive attitudes upon which our identity as individuals depends: ' ... we should think, ..., of the kind of importance we attach to the attitudes and intentions towards us of those who stand in these [personal] relationships to us, and of the kinds of *reactive* attitudes and feelings to which we ourselves are prone.' (Strawson, 1962, p. 6) Or, to put the same idea otherwise, in the making and sustaining of our identity, we really take other human beings seriously: 'My attitude towards him is an attitude towards a soul.' (Wittgenstein, 1953, II, iv)

The *recognition* by others which we get or which is withheld from us expresses their *evaluative attitudes* towards our identity and character. Herein resides, I think, a first step towards a Wittgensteinian solution of the problem of normativity. This is so because keeping in view the social dependence of a person's identity is tantamount to bearing in mind that a person identifies himself with the pro- and contra-attitudes of other people and that he subsequently takes these attitudes towards his own motivational structure. That is to say, a person's valuation system in terms of which he evaluates his own desires and preferences is basically constituted by the valuation system of the community he lives in. The socio-psychological mechanism behind such a form of self-evalution can, as already maintained and detailed in chapter four, be explained in terms of what Charles Horton Cooley (1902, p. 184) called the idea of the *reflected* or *looking-glass self.* The self-image of a person is the reflected image of him in the eyes of other people.

Now we *need* this recognition (or even misrecognition) by others in order to evaluate ourselves, primarily because of the decline of traditional hierarchical society in which ascribed social roles fixed a person's identity once and for all (Taylor, 1991, p. 47). When traditional religious and political frameworks collapse, as is the case in modernity, we have to appeal to the authority of other people to keep our mental sanity and an appropriate sense of our identity. Without the evaluative attitudes of other people we should be completely in the dark as to our *true* or *real* personal worth. Our self-esteem has to keep track of the esteem of others. Briefly, the emergence of the ideal of authenticity in the age of modernity, together with the impossibility of a monological identity, create the explicit need for recognition by other people: '... the development of an ideal of inwardly generated identity gives a new and crucial importance to recognition. My own identity crucially depends on my dialogical relations with others.' (Taylor, 1991, pp. 47-48)

Consequently, if having one's own original way is reduced and degraded to a self-centred autonomy that does not acknowledge the need for recognition by others, then one of the major possibility conditions for the ideal of authenticity is itself destroyed. The denial of the social dependence of our identity and autonomy is therefore self-defeating. True authentic autonomy — the real value of oneself — requires the normative impact of other people's attitudes.

Against private significance, for horizons of significance

But does not this community view of self-evaluation imply the eradication of all creativity and the rationalization of sheer conformism? Furthermore, if the second-order attitudes of the self considered by itself are normatively impotent, what then gives the evaluative attitudes of other people a special authoritative power? Exactly why, one perhaps wonders, is it not possible to determine values and norms all by oneself? All these and similar worries in the end boil down to the one fundamental question: *Why is private significance impossible?* It is in answering this question that what I have called Taylor's anti-private significance argument finds its place (Taylor, 1991, pp. 35-41). I briefly reconstruct this central argument.

'All options are equally worthy, because they are freely chosen, and it is choice that confers worth.' (Taylor, 1991, p. 37) This soft relativism and its underlying subjectivism about value vigorously reject the impact of all valuation frameworks which transcend the self. The possibility of private significance is an evident consequence of radical individualism. On this line of thinking, the self all by itself determines its values and norms in that it fixes 'what has significance' by radically free choice, or by decision, or by just feeling that way. However, if in my self-definition and self-evaluation *anything goes*, then my identity and personal worth become insignificant or trivial. Extreme individualism is therefore self-destructive. This is so because to be significant means to be set apart or to make a difference. But if radically free choice is the crucial justifying reason, then any option is on the same level with any other option, and consequently, no one option stands apart. Before choice confers importance upon an option, all options are, *ex hypothesi*, without importance. Since valuation frameworks anterior to choice are excluded, no option is of itself more worthwhile than any other option. But if everything can in principle become significant, then nothing has any *special* significance. If everything can make a difference, then nothing actually does. If any option we choose is all right, then no one option can make a special difference. Self-chosen difference thus becomes insignificant or trivial. It is *just crazy* to think that your choice, decision or feeling can determine what is significant.

The untenable character of private significance can, as already touched upon in chapter four, be shown in still another way (Taylor, 1977). According to the hypothesis under consideration, the higher-order attitudes in a person's self-evaluation are expressive of self-chosen values. But these putative evaluative attitudes are really either only *factual* preferences or merely *arbitrary* options. The reason for this is that if there are no prior value-criteria whatsoever by reference to which a radically free choice is made, then such a choice is either based upon the strongest attraction of one preference among other alternatives, or made without regard to preferences at all. Consequently, a special normative status can never accrue to such higher-order attitudes. A radically free choice is, after all, just a wanton movement of the mind without any special authority. Here self-determining freedom or radical autonomy collapses into *anomy* and thus the initial problem of normativity reappears again.

In sum, a single individual, considered by himself and in isolation, cannot just by *fiat* constitute normative significance because whatever is going to *seem* significant to him *ipso facto is* significant. But that only means that we cannot talk about *significance* at all. Interestingly, this parallels Wittgenstein's conclusion regarding the impossibility of private meaning (as sense) and rule-following:

> And hence also 'obeying a rule' is a practice. And to *think* one is obeying a rule is not to obey a rule. Hence it is not possible to obey a rule 'privately': otherwise thinking one was obeying a rule would be the same thing as obeying it. (Wittgenstein, 1953, I, § 202; see also § 258)

Taylor's anti-private significance argument has as an important consequence that in my self-definition and self-evaluation I have to take as a background a sense of what is significant *independent of my autonomous will*. My identity and personal worth only take on importance against a background of intelligibility or what Taylor (1991, p. 37) calls a *horizon of signifi-*

144

cance. Such a horizon is a valuation system of a historically grown community. It consists of the authoritative principles, rules, values and norms which are expressive of the normative and socially prevalent conception of the good life. Such inescapable frameworks within which we define ourselves and determine our self-worth are not chosen but discovered: 'Horizons [of significance] are given.' (Taylor, 1991, p. 39)

Of course, this line of thought immediately brings another famous remark of Wittgenstein to mind: 'What has to be accepted, the given, is — so one could say — *forms of life.*' (Wittgenstein, 1953, II, xi) If there is some truth in my suggestion that Taylor basically offers an anti-private significance argument, then forms of life are indeed necessary for authentic personal autonomy:

> Otherwise put, I can define my identity only against the background of things that matter [a horizon of significance]. ... Only if I exist in a world in which history, or the demands of nature, or the needs of my fellow human beings, or the duties of citizenship, or the call of God, or something else of this order *matters* crucially, can I define an identity for myself that is not trivial. (Taylor, 1991, pp. 40-41)

Consequently, if being true to oneself is reduced and degraded to a self-centred autonomy that shuts out horizons of significance, then another of the very possibility conditions of the ideal of authenticity is itself destroyed. Since authenticity presupposes significance, and since the constitution of significance ultimately depends upon forms of life, it follows that authenticity necessarily requires valuation frameworks which transcend the self. True authentic autonomy — the real value of oneself — requires the normative impact of what George Herbert Mead (1934, p. 154) called 'the generalized other'.

Finally, in order to further indicate the direction in which the distinctively Wittgensteinian answer to the question of normativity leads, we can bring the two parts of the community view of authenticity and self-evaluation — namely, the recognition by others and horizons of significance — briefly together. For an adequate self-evaluation a person needs the recognition of other people. His identity and self-esteem crucially depend upon their evaluative attitudes. But, of course, in their measured evaluation of a person's character, concrete other people do not express their own idiosyncratic values, but the valuation framework of the community at large. The authority of other people's evaluative attitudes is only *derivative from* the authority of the community's horizon of significance or form of life.

Now this highest court of appeal has an original or special normative status because it *transcends* a person's evaluation of himself as well as the other people's evaluation of him. Horizons of significance not only transcend the self *but also the other*. The fact that horizons are given at least means that they have some sort of dynamic life of their own. The status of such a transcendent valuation framework can, in keeping with the Wittgensteinian spirit, partially be clarified by saying that a horizon of significance is neither a relativistic or conventionalistic framework in a Humpty-Dumpty sense nor an absolute or separated framework in a Platonic sense. A form of life in so far as it pertains to common principles, rules, values and norms is a normative framework which is neither fully immanent nor strongly transcendent. A horizon of significance refers to *inherited traditions and customs* of valuing to which both the person who asks for recognition and the other people who give or deny it are subordinated. The authenticity of the self is therefore constituted against an inherited background of intelligibility by an 'ongoing conversation' between the self and the other.

The community view of authentic personal autonomy

Let me collect the results of my discussion up to this point. Although *social dependence* is usually regarded as incompatible with personal autonomy, this dependence on other people's opinions and social frameworks is, as the community view developed above demonstrates, not so much an impediment as it is a *constitutive* contribution to authentic autonomy. Admittedly, my construction of a Wittgensteinian outlook on personal autonomy in terms of Frankfurt's hierarchical model of the self and Taylor's moral psychology only offers a rough sketch of a perspicuous representation of this highly important existential and moral issue. But if there is some truth in my sketchy *übersichtliche Darstellung*, then the central claim of the community view that social factors are essential for the constitution of truly authentic autonomy seems plausible.

The community view of authentic personal autonomy justifies, I submit, the second part of my moderately heteronomous view, namely social self-evaluation. It directly follows from this view that the process of self-evaluation depends in an important sense on the normative impact of other people's attitudes. In addition, Charles Taylor's community view — his Wittgensteinian moral psychology — offers supplementary evidence for the hybrid thesis as well as the asymmetrical dependency thesis in the conceptual analysis of personal autonomy, as these theses were expounded at the end of the previous chapter.[15] By focusing on the need for recognition by

---

15. Still more additional evidence for hybridity as well as asymmetrical dependency can be found in Tugendhat (1986).

other people and establishing an anti-private significance argument, he contrasts (the ideal of) authenticity with (radical) self-determination and, furthermore, shows how the latter asymmetrically depends upon the former. That is to say, Taylor's community view corroborates the twofold doctrine that the concept of being true to oneself comprises both autonomy as (more) active self-determination by radically free choice or rational decision and authenticity as (more) passive social dependence or conformism; and, furthermore, that autonomy thus defined asymmetrically depends upon the ideal of authenticity.

However, the fact that it is possible to adequately formulate a Wittgensteinian outlook on personal autonomy and to use it as a justification for my own moderately heteronomous view, does not mean in and of itself that such an outlook is also a *justifiable* position to take in contemporary analytic anthropology. In particular, a Wittgensteinian philosophy seems at first sight to be exposed to the objection of *inherent conservatism* or *conformism*. To lower the temperature of this steamy issue, I will give two concise but important replies.

Firstly, the Wittgensteinian outlook on personal autonomy only offers a *formal* and *structural* anthropological view which belongs to an adequate account of the metaphysics of personhood. As such it remains *neutral* with regard to the particular moral and political contents which are conferred upon the formal possibility conditions of authenticity in a particular society. Horizons of significance and dialogical relationships are present in 'nice' or democratic as well as in 'grim' or totalitarian societies. There is nothing intrinsically conservative about the structural possibility conditions of authenticity.

Secondly, and more importantly, the significance *itself* of being critical of and opposed to the demands of external conformity crucially depends upon a *wider* horizon of significance that promotes authentic self-realization and self-fulfilment as worthy ideals. As the anti-private significance argument shows, the very sense of criticism and opposition presupposes the value of a *tradition* of critique. In primitive and closed societies there is not even the possibility of being critical; only in our modern Western society is such a possibility created and preserved. Even the capacity for being critical is then not something that a single individual, considered by himself and in isolation, could bring about and continue to maintain. Since criticism and opposition depend upon a community view there is nothing inherently conformistic about this view.

The ideal of authenticity

It goes without saying that personal autonomy (or authenticity) is one of the most important moral and political ideals, if not the most important one. In conclusion, I will therefore briefly explore, in the light of what went before, the role of personal autonomy and authenticity in a moral and political setting. The ideal of autonomy has played a pivotal role in the defence of individualist liberalism (Rawls, 1971; Ackerman, 1980). This close relationship between autonomy and moral or political theory is, however, contested in contemporary political philosophy (Mulhall and Swift, 1996). Mainly under the influence of feminism (Friedman, 2000) and communitarianism (Sandel, 1982), critics have launched a staunch attack on autonomy, self-control and strength of will as worthy ideals and, in place of these, they have tried to establish commitment, love and care as the primary values. Against the ideas of liberal rationalism, philosophers such as Richard Rorty, Alasdair McIntyre and Charles Taylor have engaged in critiques of conceptions of rational decision-making and free choice deriving from the philosophical enlightenment. In this chapter, I have especially dealt with Taylor's community — or, as will become clear below, *moderately* communitarian — approach to this issue and its implications for the distinction between autonomy and authenticity. Let me draw some further conclusions of my discussion for the *importance* of personal autonomy and authenticity.

The Wittgensteinian outlook on personal autonomy which I tentatively constructed in this chapter leads up to the following overall definition of authenticity in terms of Taylor's chiefly communitarian approach:

> Briefly, we can say that authenticity [on the one hand] (A) involves (i) creation and construction as well as discovery, (ii) originality, and frequently (iii) opposition to the rules of society and even potentially to what we recognize as morality. But it is also true, as we saw, that it [on the other hand] (B) requires (i) openness to horizons of significance ... and (ii) a self-definition in dialogue. That these demands may be in tension has to be allowed. But what must be wrong is a simple privileging of one over the other, of [the active dimension] (A), say, at the expense of [the passive dimension] (B), or vice versa. (Taylor, 1991, p. 66)

From this perspective, what appears wrong with much contemporary theory and practice in the liberalist tradition is indeed that they stress the *creative* or *active* dimension (A), while underplaying the receptive or passive dimension (B). Proponents of individualist liberalism start from what they take to

148

be the self-evident principle that persons are either actual or potential autonomous beings in the *radical* sense. These liberals certainly do not deny the temporal and factual dependence of autonomy on the impact of other people's attitudes and the larger communal context. But they nevertheless presume that the individual person remains *in principle* the independent creator of his volitional character as well as his values. However, if Taylor's mainly communitarian claims are plausible, then this exclusive emphasis on the self-determining freedom of persons — the exaltation of the active (A) over the passive dimension (B) — is unwarranted and even self-defeating. That is to say, if Taylor's anti-private significance argument is valid, any conception of being true to oneself which staves off horizons of significance and dialogical relationships becomes fundamentally distorted or corrupt.

On this view then, the ideal in moral practice and the starting-point of political theory cannot be personal autonomy of the radical self-determining type, but *must* be authenticity in the above-defined sense. The fundamental ideal in the moral or political field is thus not so much autonomy, as it is authenticity. So liberals cannot be right when they put an exclusive and one-dimensional emphasis on personal autonomy of the radical self-determining type. This constitutes, I think, a fruitful and promising result of an applied Wittgensteinian philosophy with regard to the moral and political domain. Of course, those in sympathy with Taylor's broadly communitarian approach to authenticity should guard against the opposite failure, namely the privileging of the *receptive* or passive dimension at the expense of the creative or active dimension. Especially feminists and communitarians are prone to this opposite exaggeration. In view of Taylor's analysis, they might better opt for a more *moderately* communitarian approach which acknowlededges, firstly, that the concept of being true to oneself comprises both autonomy as (more) active self-determination by radically free choice or rational decision and authenticity as (more) passive social dependence or conformism; and, secondly, that autonomy thus defined asymmetrically depends upon the ideal of authenticity. In other words, moderate communitarianism subscribes to the hybrid theory of personal autonomy and the attendant asymmetrical dependency thesis. At least two consequences for feminist and communitarian moral and political philosophies then follow.

Firstly, feminist and communitarian critiques of autonomy as a moral and political ideal are not so much directed at being true to oneself as such, as they are opposed to a specific construal of this, namely, as based upon radically free choice or rational decision. It has to be admitted that these critiques of autonomy as a moral or political ideal are often justified in the light of the fact that in liberalism having one's own original way is too readily *reduced* to autonomous free choice or rational decision to the neglect of those aspects of authenticity which involve social dependence and conformism. To be sure, if the asymmetrical dependency of autonomy on authenticity is true, then such a reduction is radically misguided because active autonomy cannot stand on its own. Yet feminists and communitarians must be careful not to throw the baby away with the bath water. They can perfectly well also subscribe to active autonomy as *one* important ideal, provided that being true to oneself consists of both autonomy as self-determination *and* authenticity as involving social dependence, and that the asymmetrical dependency of the former on the latter is recognized. The basic conception of being true to oneself — authenticity — remains wide enough to include such crucial elements as emotional attachment in caring and belonging to a community.

Secondly, and connectedly, the liberal values of self-control and strength of will are perfectly compatible with the feminist and communitarian values of care and commitment, as long as the former are viewed as a function of the latter in the sense that, for example, a person can only find the willpower to make certain substantial choices and decisions if he is guided by his own fundamental concerns and devotions. Not only can we have these two sets of values, in our moral and public life, we should have both. But the *way* in which we have them is all-important. In the light of the asymmetrical dependency of autonomy on authenticity the values of care and commitment are primary: liberal values are in this way derivative from feminist and communitarian values. And although feminists and communitarians are for the most part right in seeking recognition of an important receptive dimension, they must not forget to respect *the fundamental tension* in the ideal of authenticity between being active and being passive, for such a tension belongs to the very nature of the self.

Appendix
The Memory Theory of Personal Identity

Introduction

As said in chapter one, the memory theory is part of the empiricist mental continuity theory of personal identity through time. In this appendix I discuss this historically important memory theory and its technical difficulties in more detail.

Personal identity and experiential memory

The pertinent identity question is: What unites person-phases at different moments into one and the same consciousness through time? What makes these phases 'co-conscious' or 'co-personal'? Which unity relation constitutes the history of the empirical self? The most obvious unity relation for persons is the *memory* relation, for it is in our memory that we have a privileged access to our own identity. Indeed, who would we be without memories? Our identity is inescapably bound up with our memory. Although in certain cases person A might use diaries or photo albums to know what he has experienced or accomplished, in most cases A does not need to make an appeal to such an indirect procedure in order to discover his identity. Most of the time A remembers who he was in an immediate, direct manner. It is hardly surprising, then, that empiricists began analyzing personal identity through time in terms of memory. The pioneer of the memory theory of personal identity through time was John Locke:

> ..., since consciousness always accompanies thinking, and it is that which makes every one to be what he calls self, and thereby distinguishes himself from all other thinking things: in this alone consists personal identity, i.e., the sameness of a rational being; and as far as this consciousness can be extended backwards to any past action or thought, so far reaches the identity of that person; it is the same self now it was then; and

151

it is by the same self with this present one that now reflects on
it, that that action was done. (Locke, 1694, pp. 39-40)

The 'consciouness [that] can be extended backwards to any past action or
thought' is Locke's unwieldy formula for the faculty of memory, i.e. reflective awareness of experiences, actions and events in the past. On Locke's
view, then, it is our memories that determine the extension of our identity.

Not just any memories, however, are important for an analysis of the
nature of personal identity. The memories that constitute our identity are
memories of personal experiences. This so-called *experiential memory* must
be distinguished from factual memory and habitual memory.[1] The theoretical memory of facts — remembering *that* — and the practical memory of
habits — remembering *how* — are both impersonal memories: impersonal
in the sense that they are not the special characteristic of a particular person.
Many different people remember that Napoleon was defeated in 1814 at
Waterloo and how to drive a car. 'Remembering that' and 'remembering
how' are not especially individuating: they do not pick out any particular
person. Only a memory of a personal experience can do that. This is so
because memory *of* personal experiences is memory of experiences that fall
within one's own personal biography. I do indeed remember that Napoleon
was defeated in 1814 at Waterloo, but not Napoleon being defeated. If it
would be the case that I could remember Napoleon being defeated, that
would imply that I had *personal* experiences of that event. To remember personal experiences is to remember *having* those experiences. I can remember
other people's experiences, but I cannot remember their having those experiences. I only remember the experiences of others 'from the outside'; my
own experiences I remember 'from the inside'. These personal memories are
reported in a typical manner: 'I remember *having* this-or-that experience' or
'I remember *experiencing* such-and-such'.

What constitutes personal identity through time, according to the memory theory, is experiential memory. The memory of having experience *e*
forges a constitutive connection between the person who now remembers
experience *e* from the inside and the person who had experience *e* in the
past: they are one and the same person. Or put in terms of person-phases:
two person-phases belong to one and the same personal history if and only

---

1. This distinction is analogous to the distinction between 'knowledge *of*', 'knowledge *that*'
   and 'knowledge *how*' in epistemology. This analogy is no coincidence since memory is
   one of our most important sources of knowledge, especially of knowledge of the past.
   See, Shoemaker, 1967. A synonym for 'experiential memory' is *event memory*: memories
   of events in personal life. Under experiential memory one could also group memories of
   performing personal (speech) acts. Empiricists reduce these external events to *internal* personal experiences.

if they are connected by the relation of experiential memory, i.e., when the later person-phase *actually* contains a memory of an experience that the earlier person-phase contained. For reasons of economy, in what follows 'memory' will indicate experiential memory and 'memory connectedness' will indicate the unity relation of actual experiential memory connectedness. In short, the necessary and sufficient ontological condition for personal identity through time is, according to the memory theory:

> (MT) person X today is one and the same person as person Y at a particular moment in the past if and only if there exists *memory connectedness* between X and Y.

The attempt to analyze what it is that constitutes personal identity through time in terms of memory connectedness runs up against three fundamental difficulties: (i) the problem of circularity, (ii) the problem of actuality and (iii) the problem of absurdity. The former two have to do with the concept of memory, the latter one with the relation of connectedness. The empiricist project of analyzing personal identity without appealing to 'the subject of experiences' can only succeed when these obstacles have been removed. This implies considerable technical amendments to the crude identity condition in terms of memory connectedness.

The problem of circularity

One fundamental criticism of the attempt to analyze personal identity in terms of memory argues that such an analysis is circular: personal identity cannot, without circularity, be analyzed in terms of memory since a full and correct analysis of the concept of memory *presupposes* personal identity. Joseph Butler was the first to have made this point: 'And one should really think it self-evident, that consciousness of personal identity presupposes, and therefore cannot constitute, personal identity, any more than knowledge, in any other case, can constitute truth, which it presupposes.' (Butler, 1736, p. 100)

The critic asserts the following. Memories are typically reported thus: 'I remember having experience *e*'. Now I can remember someone else's experience, but I cannot remember having someone else's experience. My memory of having had an experience is always memory of *my* having had that experience. The full and correct report of memory then becomes: 'I remember *my* having experience *e*'. In other words, it is a conceptual truth that we can only remember *our own* experiences 'from the inside'. As a consequence, memory connectedness presupposes personal identity since personal identity is a part of the full and correct analysis of memory. So, as maintained by the critic, it cannot be the result of the analysis of memory.

A proponent of the memory theory of personal identity can, however, escape the problem of circularity by introducing the concept of *quasi*-memory or q-memory for short. This concept is an extension of the concept of memory as a causal concept. The necessity of construing the memory concept as a causal concept must therefore first be demonstrated.

When do we say that I *remember* having experience *e*? According to the non-causal concept of memory we can say:

> 'I remember having experience *e*' if and only if (1) I apparently remember having experience *e* and (2) I had experience *e* (Shoemaker, 1959).

Call the latter condition the 'witness condition': I was a witness to my having experience *e*. It is this witness condition which guarantees that my apparent memories are not illusory but real memories. If I was not a witness to my having experience *e*, then my apparently remembering having experience *e* is not a real memory; I only just imagine my having had experience *e*.

These two conditions are not, however, sufficient to be able to say that I really remember having experience *e*. Both conditions can be fulfilled without my *remembering* having experience *e*. It is possible that (1) my apparent memory of having experience *e* has been induced by post-hypnotic suggestion and only coincidentally agrees with (2) my having experience *e* in the past, an event which I have completely forgotten. In such a case one would not say that I really remember having experience *e*. Nor would one say that in the case where (1) my apparent memory of having experience *e* is the result of the following sequence of events: (2) my having experience *e* in the past; then totally forgetting that I had experience *e*; then learning (again), for example by hearsay (my mother told me), that I had experience *e*; then my impeccably imagining that I had experience *e*; and finally my seeming to remember having experience *e*.

As a third condition, my memory of having experience *e* requires that my apparent memory of having experience *e* be *caused* in an *appropriate* manner, namely by my having experience *e* in the past. It must not be caused by post-hypnotic suggestion or by hearsay and imagination. The addition of a necessary 'causal condition' to the analysis of memory marks the concept of memory as a *causal* concept (Martin and Deutscher, 1966; Wollheim, 1979). According to the causal analysis of memory we can say:

'I remember having experience e' if and only if ($1'$) I apparently remember having experience e; ($2'$) *I* had experience e; and ($3'$) my apparent memory of having experience e is caused in an appropriate way by *my* having experience e in the past.

Of course, an analysis of personal identity on the basis of this causal concept of memory is just as circular as one based on the non-causal concept of memory. This is why the personal and possessive pronouns (*I* and *my*) are italicized. One can, however, escape the circularity on the basis of the causal condition, for this condition makes possible the introduction of the concept of q-memory, a concept that can be analyzed *without* relying on the concept of personal identity (Shoemaker, 1970). According to the causal analysis of q-memory we can say:

'I q-remember having experience e' if and only if ($1"$) I apparently remember having experience e; ($2"$) *someone* had experience e; and ($3"$) my apparent memory of having experience e is caused in an appropriate way by *someone* having experience e in the past.

Since anyone could have had experience e, a less unwieldy formulation of the causal condition is possible:

($3"$) my apparent memory of experience e is caused in an appropriate way by experience e which occured in the past.

It is now this third, causal condition which guarantees that my apparent memories are not illusory but real memories. *I myself* do not necessarily have to fulfill the witness condition in order to really remember experiences that occurred in the past. As long as my apparent memories are causally dependent, in the right kind of way, on past experiences, I really remember those experiences whether or not I had them myself.

It is then the causal condition which succeeds in erasing personal identity in the q-memory process: q-memories do *not* presuppose personal identity. So the causal condition of q-memory makes it possible to counter the objection that personal identity is a part of the full and correct analysis of memory. Now the normal concept of memory presupposes that we can remember only our own experiences 'from the inside'. Yet one consequence of the concept of q-memory is the logical possibility that we can q-remember *someone else's* experiences 'from the inside'.[2] A further consequence of the q-analysis is that our normal memories are special cases of q-memories: a normal memory is a q-memory of one's own experience. The basic concept, then, is that of q-memory.

This q-analysis of remembering — and of mental concepts in general — suggests something that is even more radical and bolder: the *impersonal* analysis of experiences (Parfit, 1984, pp. 225-226). Since the identity of the person or persons has no importance in the causal analysis of the relations between experiences, such an analysis can also be carried out entirely impersonally, i.e. without any reference to persons. Relations between experiences can by analyzed in a manner that does not assume that these experiences are had by persons, that they belong to 'subjects of experiences'. On the causal analysis of impersonal memory, for example, we can say:

> 'a memory of a past experience *e* occurs' if and only if (1^*) an apparent memory of experience *e* occurs; (2^*) an experience *e* occured; and (3^*) the apparent memory is caused in an appropriate way by experience *e* which occured in the past.

The same analysis holds *mutatis mutandis* for impersonal intention, impersonal character traits, impersonal beliefs and desires, etc. Although, for example, Parfit needs this impersonal analysis of experiences for the defence of his reductionist solution to the problem of personal identity (chapter two), such an audacious analysis is not needed for the solution of the empiricist problem of circularity; it suffices to have the q-analysis.

Armed with the concept of q-memory, the empiricist can escape the problem of circularity posed by his crude memory theory of personal identity, since q-memory connectedness does *not* presuppose personal identity. This means that personal identity can be analyzed in terms of q-memory without running the risk of circularity. Personal identity then appears as a consequence of, not as a part of, the analysis of q-memory connectedness.[3] A first fundamental amendment to the necessary and sufficient ontological condition for personal identity through time, as stated by the empiricist memory theory, can now be formulated:

---

2. Of course, this possibility has not (yet) been realized. But in the imaginary case of *reduplication*, q-remembering someone else's experiences is just as common as remembering one's own experiences. For the thought-experiment of reduplication, see chapter two.
3. This is so, according to the empiricist, with the additional condition that the q-memory-connectedness does *not* take a *branching* form as is the case with reduplication. For the non-branching condition, see again chapter two.

(MT-1) person X today is one and the same person as person Y at a particular moment in the past if and only if there exists *q-memory connectedness* between X and Y.

The problem of actuality

There is, however, still another obstacle related to this q-amendment, one having to do with the fact that persons are not constantly in an actual state of q-memory. This additional difficulty is also associated with the concept of memory: we do not permanently remember our entire life. Persons do not actually remember all their experiences all the time. Thomas Reid was the first to have pointed out this simple problem of actuality: 'As our consciousness sometimes ceases to exist, as in sound sleep, our personal identity must cease with it.' (Reid, 1785b, p. 118) This is clear in the case of person A who is asleep and also in the case of person B who is suffering from a (temporary) loss of memory. Sleeping A is not q-memory-connected with awake A. B's amnesia person-phase contains no q-memories of experiences which are contained by earlier person-phases of B. A asleep, or B suffering memory loss, is therefore, according to the above-mentioned identity condition (MT-1), not one and the same person as A awake or B not suffering memory loss.

When we move from actual to *possible* q-memories, however, this obstacle can be avoided (Perry, 1975c). Although A asleep does not actually q-remember the experiences of A awake, A asleep *can* q-remember them, for example, when A is awakened and asked about it. In other words, we make an appeal to A's dispositional memory. Although B suffering memory loss does not actually q-remember the experiences of B not suffering memory loss, B's amnesia person-phase *would* contain, given certain conditions, q-memories of experiences which are contained by earlier person-phases of B, for example, if B had not had a car accident and had been asked about it. That is to say, we make an appeal to B's conditional (or counterfactual) memory.

We are now in a position to make a second additional amendment on behalf of the empiricist memory theory of personal identity, and restate the necessary and sufficient identity condition thus:

(MT-2) person X today is one and the same person as person Y at a particular moment in the past if and only if there exists *possible q-memory connectedness* between X and Y.

For reasons of economy, in what follows 'memory connectedness' will always mean possible q-memory connectedness.

The problem of absurdity

The introduction of possible q-memories does not, however, solve all the problems for the empiricist. It is a common fact that people *completely forget* some parts of their lives; they can radically lose memories forever. For most of us, it is just impossible to remember all of our life; there just are no possible memories left of some periods in our life. This phenomenon of radical forgetting leads to absurdities when memory connectedness is proposed as a condition for personal identity, as stated by (MT-2).

Reid was the first to have pointed out the absurdity of the memory theory, using the 'paradox of the brave officer' (Reid, 1785b). Imagine that a person is punished as a young boy for stealing apples. He remembers this years later when he is decorated for his brave deeds as a young officer. And he remembers this decoration years later as an old general, but by then he has completely forgotten his punishment for stealing the apples. It is impossible for the old general to remember this event. Neither psychoanalysis nor hypnosis provide the slightest result.

Now according to the unity relation of memory connectedness, as stated by the memory theory (MT-2), the young officer is one and the same person as the boy and the old general is one and the same person as the young officer, but the old general is not one and the same person as the boy. This is absurd because consistent with the transitivity of identity — if $X = Y$ and $Y = Z$ then $X = Z$ — the old general must be one and the same person as the boy. In other words, the memory theory has the absurd consequence: '... that a man may be, and at the same time not be, the person that did a particular action.' (Reid, 1785b, pp. 114-115)

The unity relation for persons must be transitive because of the transitivity of the identity relation. The unity relation of memory connectedness is *not* transitive; the paradox of the brave officer shows that it is not useful as an identity condition. The empiricists solve this typical difficulty for the crude memory theory by drawing a distinction between *direct* and *indirect* memory connectedness (Quinton, 1962, pp. 58-59). Direct memory connectedness is intransitive, whereas indirect memory connectedness is transitive. When X is directly memory-connected with Y and Y is directly memory-connected with Z, this does not necessarily mean that X is then also directly memory-connected with Z. The old general does not remember what he did as a boy. One can, however, appeal to indirect memory connectedness, i.e. a relation that is composed of direct memory links. If X is directly memory-

158

related with Y and Y is directly memory-related with Z, then X is indirectly memory-related to Z.

Now a memory theory that analyzes personal identity through time in terms of indirect memory connectedness escapes the paradox of the brave officer. The effectiveness of the relation of indirect memory connectedness can best be seen when we use the terminology of person-phases. Two person-phases are directly memory-connected if the later phase contains memories of experiences that the earlier one contained. And two person-phases are indirectly memory-connected if they are the endpoints of a series of person-phases within which each person-phase is directly memory-connected with the previous one. In the paradox of the brave officer we have only one mediating link, but there can in principle be a great number of mediating links constituting the chain of indirect memory connectedness.

This relation of indirect memory connectedness is called the relation of continuity of memories or *memory continuity* for short. The relation of memory continuity is to the relation of memory connectedness as the relation '*a* is an ancestor of *b*' to the relation '*a* is the father of *b*': memory continuity is the *ancestral* relation of memory connectedness. Just as X's grandfather is X's ancestor but not X's father, so X's person-phase as a child is memory-continuous but not memory-connected with X's person-phase as an old man. Memory continuity, then, consists of an uninterrupted chain of overlapping links of (direct) memory connectedness. Memory continuity can be a candidate for the unity relation for persons because it is transitive: if there exists memory continuity both between X and Y and between Y and Z, then there also exists memory continuity between X and Z. We are now in a position to formulate, on behalve of the empiricist memory theory, a third fundamental amendment to the necessary and sufficient ontological condition for personal identity through time:

> (MT-3) person X today is one and the same person as person Y at a particular moment in the past if and only if there exists *memory continuity* between X and Y (and memory continuity is a chain of overlapping links of memory connectedness).

If we unpack again the full content of what was put in the 'memory'-box before, then we can reformulate (MT-3) as follows:

> (MT') person X today is one and the same person as person Y at a particular moment in the past if and only if there exists *continuity of possible experiential q-memory* between X and Y

(and this continuity is a chain of overlapping links of possible experiential q-memory connectedness).

Memory and mental continuity

At this point, the difficulties of an empiricist memory theory have been surmounted: memory continuity — that is to say, the continuity of possible experiential q-memory (MT') — as the unity relation for persons is the sophisticated final result. In this appendix I discussed the memory theory and its difficulties at lenght because this theory provides the model for a *broader* empiricist theory of personal identity through time, namely the mental continuity theory, of which I give an account in chapter one.

On the empiricist mental continuity theory, self-identity is not only constituted by experiential memories. Who we are is also determined by other mental qualities: our character, our intentions, our desires, our beliefs, etc. Experiential memories make up part of a broader identity-constituting *mental* complex. Yet they will continue to play a central role in the constitution of identity. This is so because their identifying and individuating capacity is much more powerful than that of character traits, intentions, desires, beliefs, etc. More than one person can have qualitatively identical characters, desires, etc., whereas my detailed experiential memories are exclusively my own possession.

Bibliography

Ackerman, B. (1980), *Social Justice and the Liberal State*, Yale University Press, New Haven.

Albritton, R. (1985), 'Freedom of Will and Freedom of Action', *Proceedings and Addresses of the American Philosophical Association*, vol. 59, pp.239-51.

Anscombe, G.E.M. (1975), 'The First Person', in Anscombe, G.E.M., *Metaphysics and the Philosophy of Mind. The Collected Philosophical Papers of G.E.M. Anscombe, Volume Two*, Basil Blackwell, Oxford, 1981, pp.21-36.

Armstrong, D.M. (1978), 'What is Consiousness?', in Armstrong D.M., *The Nature of Mind and Other Essays*, Cornell University Press, Ithaca, 1981, pp.55-67.

Ayer, A.J. (1963), 'The Concept of a Person', in Ayer, A.J., *The Concept of a Person and Other Essays*, Macmillan, London, pp.82-128.

Biletzki, A. and Matar, A. (eds) (1998), *The Story of Analytic Philosophy. Plot and Heroes*, Routledge, London.

Blackburn, S. (1998), *Ruling Passions. A Theory of Practical Reasoning*, Clarendon Press, Oxford.

Butler, J. (1736), 'Of Personal Identity', in Perry, J. (ed.), *Personal Identity*, University of California Press, Berkeley, 1975, pp.99-105.

Campbell, J. (1994), *Past, Space, and Self*, The MIT Press, Cambridge, Massachusetts.

Carrithers, M., Collins, S. and Lukes, S. (1985), *The Category of the Person. Anthropology, Philosophy, History*, Cambridge University Press, Cambridge.

Cassam, Q. (1997), *Self and World*, Clarendon Press, Oxford.

Chisholm, R.M. (1969), 'The Loose and Popular and the Strict and Philosophical Senses of Identity', in Care, N.S. and Grimm, R.H., *Perception and Personal Identity*, The Press of Case Western Reserve University, Cleveland, pp.82-106.

Chisholm, R.M. (1970a), 'Identity Through Time', in Kiefer, H. and Munitz, M. (eds), *Language, Belief and Metaphysics*, State University of New York Press, New York, pp.163-182.

Chisholm, R.M. (1970b), 'Reply to Strawsons Comments', in Kiefer H. and Munitz, M., *Language, Belief and Metaphysics*, State University of New York Press, New York, pp.187-189.

Chisholm, R.M. (1976), *Person and Object. A Metaphysical Study,* George Allen and Unwin, London.

Christman, J. (1989), 'Introduction', in Christman, J. (ed.), *The Inner Citadel. Essays on Individual Autonomy,* Oxford University Press, Oxford, pp.3-23.

Churchland, P.M. (1986), 'The Continuity of Philosophy and the Sciences', *Mind and Language,* vol. 1, pp.5-14.

Coburn, R.C. (1985), 'Personal Identity Revisited', *Canadian Journal of Philosophy,* vol. 15, pp.379-403.

Cockburn, D. (1990), *Other Human Beings,* MacMillan, London.

Cooley, C.H. (1902), *Human Nature and the Social Order,* Transaction Books, New Brunswick, 1983.

Cuypers, S.E. (1995), 'Philosophy of Mind', in Blommaert, J., Östman, J.O. and Verschueren, J. (eds), *Handbook of Pragmatics, Manual,* John Benjamins Publishing Company, Amsterdam/Philadelphia, pp.414-418.

Cuypers, S.E. (1998a), 'Philosophical Atomism and the Metaphysics of Personal Identity', *International Philosophical Quarterly,* vol. XXXVIII, pp.349-368.

Cuypers, S.E. (1998b), 'Robust Activity, Event-Causation, and Agent-Causation', in J. Bransen and S.E. Cuypers (eds), *Human Action, Deliberation and Causation,* Kluwer Academic Publishers, Dordrecht/Boston/London, pp.271-294.

Cuypers, S.E. (2000), 'Autonomy beyond Voluntarism: In Defense of Hierarchy', *Canadian Journal of Philosophy,* vol. 30, pp.225-256.

Dancy, J. (1985), *An Introduction to Contemporary Epistemology,* Basil Blackwell, Oxford.

Davidson, D. (1980), *Essays on Actions and Events,* Clarendon Press, Oxford.

Davidson, D. (1982), 'Rational Animals', *Dialectica,* vol. 36, pp.317-327.

Davidson, D. (1984), *Inquiries into Truth and Interpretation,* Clarendon Press, Oxford.

Dennett, D.C. (1971), 'Intentional Systems', in Dennett, D.C., *Brainstorms. Philosophical Essays on Mind and Psychology,* The Harvester Press, Brighton, 1981, pp.3-22.

Dennett, D.C. (1976), 'Conditions of Personhood', in Dennett, D.C., *Brainstorms. Philosophical Essays on Mind and Psychology,* The Harvester Press, Brighton, 1981, pp.267-285.

Dennett, D.C. (1978), 'Introduction', in Dennett, D.C., *Brainstorms. Philosophical Essays on Mind and Psychology,* The Harvester Press, Brighton, 1981, pp.i-xxii.

Dennett, D.C. and Douglas, R.H. (eds) (1982), *The Mind's I. Fantasies and Reflections on Self and Soul,* Bantam Books, Toronto.

Descartes, R. (1641), *Meditations on First Philosophy,* in Cottingham, et. al. (eds), *The Philosophical Works of Descartes, Volume Two,* Cambridge University Press, Cambridge, 1991.

Dworkin, G. (1981), 'The Concept of Autonomy', in Christman, J. (ed.), *The Inner*

Citadel. Essays on Individual Autonomy, Oxford University Press, Oxford, 1981, pp.54-62.

Dworkin, G. (1988), *The Theory and Practice of Autonomy*, Cambridge University Press, Cambridge.

Elster, J. (1978), *Logic and Society: Contradictions and Possible Worlds*, John Wiley and Sons, Chichester.

Elster, J. (1984), *Ulysses and the Sirens. Studies in Rationality and Irrationality. Revised Edition*, Cambridge University Press, Cambridge.

Fischer, J.M. and Ravizza, M. (1994), 'Autonomy and History', *Midwest Studies in Philosophy*, vol. XIX, pp.430-451.

Fodor, J.A. (1990), *A Theory of Content and Other Essays*, The MIT Press, Cambridge, Massachusetts.

Føllesdal, D. (1996), 'Analytic Philosophy: What Is It And Why Should One Engage In It?', *Ratio (New Series)*, vol. IX, pp.193-208.

Frankfurt, H.G. (1971), 'Freedom of the Will and the Concept of a Person', in Frankfurt, H.G., *The Importance of What We Care About*, Cambridge University Press, Cambridge, 1988, pp.11-25.

Frankfurt, H.G. (1975), 'Three Concepts of Free Action', in Frankfurt, H.G., *The Importance of What We Care About*, Cambridge University Press, Cambridge, 1988, pp.47-57.

Frankfurt, H.G. (1976), 'Identification and Externality', in Frankfurt, H.G., *The Importance of What We Care About*, Cambridge University Press, Cambridge, 1988, pp.58-68.

Frankfurt, H.G. (1978), 'The Problem of Action', in Frankfurt, H.G., *The Importance of What We Care About*, Cambridge University Press, Cambridge, 1988, pp.69-79.

Frankfurt, H.G. (1982), 'The Importance of What We Care About', in Frankfurt, H.G., *The Importance of What We Care About*, Cambridge University Press, Cambridge, 1988, pp.80-94.

Frankfurt, H.G. (1987), 'Identification and Wholeheartedness', in Frankfurt, H.G., *The Importance of What We Care About*, Cambridge University Press, Cambridge, 1988, pp.159-176.

Frankfurt, H.G. (1988a), 'Rationality and the Unthinkable', in Frankfurt, H.G., *The Importance of What We Care About*, Cambridge University Press, Cambridge, 1988, pp.177-190.

Frankfurt, H.G. (1988b), 'Preface', in Frankfurt, H.G., *The Importance of What We Care About*, Cambridge University Press, Cambridge, 1988, pp. vii-ix.

Frankfurt, H.G. (1989), 'Concerning the Freedom and Limits of the Will', in Frankfurt, H.G., *Necessity, Volition, and Love*, Cambridge University Press, Cambridge, 1999, pp.71-81.

Frankfurt, H.G. (1993), 'On the Necessity of Ideals', in Frankfurt, H.G., *Necessity,*

Volition, and Love, Cambridge University Press, Cambridge, 1999, pp.108-116.

Frankfurt, H.G. (1994), 'Autonomy, Necessity and Love', in Frankfurt, H.G., *Necessity, Volition, and Love*, Cambridge University Press, Cambridge, 1999, pp.129-141.

Friedman, M.A. (1986), 'Autonomy and the Split-Level Self', *The Southern Journal of Philosophy*, vol. 24, pp.19-35.

Friedman, M.A. (2000), 'Feminism in Ethics: Conceptions of Autonomy', in Fricker M. and Hornsby, J. (eds), *The Cambridge Companion to Feminism in Philosophy*, Cambridge University Press, Cambridge.

Grayling, A.C. (1982), *An Introduction to Philosophical Logic*, Harvester Press, Brighton.

Heidegger, M. (1927), *Being and Time*, Macquarrie, J. and Robinson, E. (transl.), Blackwell, Oxford, 1962.

Hobbes, T. (1651), *Leviathan*, Tuck, R. (ed.), Cambridge University Press, Cambridge, 1996.

Hume, D. (1739-40), *A Treatise of Human Nature*, Selby-Bigge, L.A. and Nidditch, P.H. (eds), Clarendon Press, Oxford, 1978.

Hume, D. (1739), 'Of Personal Identity', in Perry, J. (ed.), *Personal Identity*, University of California Press, Berkeley, 1975, pp.161-172.

Hume, D. (1940), 'Second Thoughts', in Perry, J. (ed.), *Personal Identity*, University of California Press, Berkeley, 1975, pp.173-176.

James, W. (1892), *Psychology: Briefer Course*, Harvard University Press, Cambridge Massachusetts, 1984.

Johnstone Jr., H.W. (1970), *The Problem of the Self*, Pennsylvania State University Press, University Park.

Kant, I. (1785), *Groundwork of the Metaphysics of Morals*, Paton, H.J. (transl.), Harper and Row, New York, 1964.

Kim, J. (1996), *Philosophy of Mind*, Westview Press, Boulder.

Kitcher, P. (1982), 'Kant's Paralogisms', *The Philosophical Review*, vol. XCI , pp.515-547.

Korsgaard, C.M. (1996), *The Sources of Normativity*, Cambridge University Press, Cambridge.

Kripke, S. (1982), *Wittgenstein on Rules and Private Language. An Elementary exposition*, Basil Blackwell, Oxford.

Lichtenberg, G.C. (1983), 'Sudelbücher' (Undatierbar: I/99,1), in Mautner, F.H (ed.), *Georg Christoph Lichtenberg. Schriften und Briefe, Band I*, Insel Verlag, Frankfurt am Main.

Locke, J. (1694), 'Of Identity and Diversity', in Perry, J. (ed.), *Personal Identity*, University of California Press, Berkeley, 1975, pp.33-52.

Lowe, E.J. (1991), 'Real Selves: Persons as a Substantial Kind', in Cockburn, D. (ed.), *Human Beings*, Cambridge University Press, Cambridge, pp.87-108.

Lyons, W. (1986), *The Disappearance of Introspection*, The MIT Press, Cambridge, Massachusetts.

MacIntyre, A. (1985), *After Virtue. A Study in Moral Theory*, Duckworth, London.

Mackie, J.L. (1976), *Problems from Locke*, Clarendon Press, Oxford.

Madell, G. (1976), 'Ayer on Personal Identity', *Philosophy*, vol. 51, pp.47-55.

Madell, G. (1981), *The Identity of the Self*, The Edinburgh University Press, Edinburgh.

Madell, G. (1989), 'Personal Identity and the Mind-Body Problem', in Smythies, J.R. and Beloff, J. (eds), *The Case for Dualism*, University Press of Virginia, Charlottesville, pp.25-41.

Malcolm, N. (1954), 'Wittgenstein's Philosophical Investigations', in Malcolm, N., *Knowledge and Certainty. Essays and Lectures*, Cornell University Press, Ithaca, 1963, pp.96-129.

Malcolm, N. (1988), 'Subjectivity', *Philosophy*, vol. 63, pp.147-160.

Martin, C.B. and Deutscher, M. (1966), 'Remembering', *The Philosophical Review*, vol. LXXV, pp.161-196.

Martin, R. and Barresi, J. (2000), *Naturalization of the Soul. Self and Personal Identity in the Eighteenth Century*, Routledge, London.

Mauss, M. (1938), 'Une Catégorie de l'Esprit Humain: la Notion de Personne, celle de "Moi"', in Mauss, M., *Sociologie et Anthropologie*, Presses Universitaires de France, Paris, 1950, pp.331-362.

McDowell, J. (1997), 'Reductionism and the First Person', in Dancy, J. (ed.), *Reading Parfit*, Blackwell, Oxford, pp.230-50.

McGinn, C. (1982), *The Character of Mind*, Oxford University Press, Oxford.

McNeill, W. and Feldman, K.S. (eds) (1998), *Continental Philosophy. An Anthology*, Blackwell, Oxford.

McTaggart, J. (1927), 'Spirit', in McTaggert, J., *The Nature of Existence, Volume II*, Cambridge University Press, Cambridge.

Mead, G.H. (1934), *Mind, Self, and Society From the Standpoint of a Social Behaviorist*, in Morris, C.W. (ed.), University of Chicago Press, Chicago, 1962.

Mele, A.R. (1992), *Springs of Action. Understanding Intentional Behavior*, Oxford University Press, Oxford.

Mounier, E. (1952), *Personalism*, University of Notre Dame Press, Notre Dame.

Mulhall, S. and Swift, A. (1996), *Liberals and Communitarians. Second Edition*, Blackwell, Oxford.

Nagel, T. (1979), *Mortal Questions*, Cambridge University Press, Cambridge.

Nagel, T. (1986), *The View from Nowhere*, Oxford University Press, Oxford.

Noonan, H.W. (1989), *Personal Identity*, Routledge, London.

Nozick, R. (1981), 'Philosophy and the Meaning of Life', in Nozick, R., *Philosophical Explanations*, The Belknap Press of Harvard University Press, Cambridge, Massachusetts, pp.571-647.

Nussbaum, M.C. (1986), *The Fragility of Goodness. Luck and Ethics in Greek Tragedy and Philosophy*, Cambridge University Press, Cambridge.

Oakeshott, M.J. (1959), 'The Voice of Poetry in the Conversation of Mankind', in Oakeshott, M.J., *Rationalism in Politics and Other Essays*, Liberty Press, Indianapolis, 1991, pp.488-541.

O'Connor, T. (ed.) (1995), *Agents, Causes, and Events. Essays on Indeterminism and Free Will*, Oxford University Press, Oxford.

Oksenberg Rorty, A. (1976) (ed.), *The Identities of Persons*, University of California Press, Berkeley.

Olsen, E.T., (1997), *The Human Animal. Personal Identity without Psychology*, Oxford University Press, New York.

Papineau, D. (1993), *Philosophical Naturalism*, Blackwell, Oxford.

Parfit, D. (1971), 'Personal Identity', in Perry, J. (ed.), *Personal Identity*, University of California Press, Berkeley, 1975, pp.199-223.

Parfit, D. (1984), *Reasons and Persons*, Clarendon Press, Oxford.

Perry, J. (1975a) (ed.), *Personal Identity*, University of California Press, Berkeley.

Perry, J. (1975b), 'The Problem of Personal Identity', in Perry, J. (ed.), *Personal Identity*, University of California Press, Berkeley, 1975, pp.3-30.

Perry, J. (1975c), 'Personal Identity, Memory, and the Problem of Circularity', in Perry, J. (ed.), *Personal Identity*, University of California Press, Berkeley, 1975, pp.135-155.

Perry, J. (1976), 'The Importance of Being Identical', in Oksenberg Rorty, A. (ed.), *The Identities of Persons*, University of California Press, Berkeley, 1976, pp.67-90.

Piper, A.M.S. (1985), 'Two Conceptions of the Self', *Philosophical Studies*, vol. 48, pp.173-97.

Quinton, A. (1962), 'The Soul', in Perry, J. (ed.), *Personal Identity*, University of California Press, Berkeley, 1975, pp.51-72.

Rawls, J. (1971), *A Theory of Justice*, Harvard University Press, Cambridge, Massachusetts.

Reid, T. (1785a), 'Of Identity', in Perry, J. (ed.), *Personal Identity*, University of California Press, Berkeley, 1975, pp.107-112.

Reid, T. (1785b), 'Of Mr. Locke's Account of Our Personal Identity', in Perry, J. (ed.), *Personal Identity*, University of California Press, Berkeley, 1975, pp.113-118.

Reid, T. (1788), *Essays on the Active Powers of the Human Mind*, Brody, B.A. (ed.), The MIT Press, Cambridge, Massachusetts, 1969.

Ricoeur, P. (1990), *Oneself as Another*, Blamey, B. (transl.), Chicago University Press, Chicago, 1992.

Rowe, W.L. (1991), 'Responsibility, Agent-Causation, and Freedom: An Eighteenth-Century View', in Fischer, J.M. and Ravizza, M. (eds), *Perspectives on Moral Responsibility*, Cornell University Press, Ithaca, 1993, pp.263-285.

Russell, B. (1912), *The Problems of Philosophy*, Oxford University Press, Oxford, 1967.

Russell, B. (1914), 'On the Nature of Acquaintance', in Russell, B., *Logic and Knowledge. Essays 1901-1950*, R.C. Marsh (ed.), Unwin Hyman, London, 1956, pp.125-174.

Russell, B. (1918), 'The Philosophy of Logical Atomism', in Russell, B., *Logic and Knowledge. Essays 1901-1950*, R.C. Marsh (ed.), Unwin Hyman, London, 1956, pp.175-281.

Russell, B. (1924), 'Logical Atomism', in Russell, B., *Logic and Knowledge. Essays 1901-1950*, R.C. Marsh (ed.), Unwin Hyman, London, 1956, pp.321-343.

Sandel, M. (1982), *Liberalism and the Limits of Justice*, Cambridge University Press, Cambridge.

Sartre, J.-P. (1948), *Existentialism and Humanism*, Mairet, P. (transl.), Methuen, London.

Schechtman, M. (1996), *The Constitution of Selves*, Cornell University Press, Ithaca.

Scheler, M. (1913-1916), *Formalism in Ethics and Non-Formal Ethics of Values. A New Attempt toward the Foundation of an Ethical Personalism*, Northwestern University Press, Evanston, 1973.

Sellars, W. (1962), 'Philosophy and the Scientific Image of Man', in Sellars, W., *Science, Perception and Reality*, Routledge and Kegan Paul, London, 1963, pp.1-40.

Shoemaker, S. (1959), 'Personal Identity and Memory', in Perry, J. (ed.), *Personal Identity*, University of California Press, Berkeley, 1975, pp.119-134.

Shoemaker, S. (1963), *Self-Knowlegde and Self-Identity*, Cornell University Press, Ithaca.

Shoemaker, S. (1967), 'Memory', in Edwards, P. (ed.), *The Encyclopedia of Philosophy, Volume V*, Macmillan, New York, pp.265-274.

Shoemaker, S. (1968), 'Self-reference and Self-awareness', in Shoemaker, S., *Identity, Cause, and Mind*, Cambridge University Press, Cambridge, 1984, pp.6-18.

Shoemaker, S. (1970), 'Persons and Their Past', in Shoemaker, S., *Identity, Cause, and Mind*, Cambridge University Press, Cambridge, 1984, pp.19-48

Shoemaker, S. (1979), 'Identity, Properties, and Causality', in Shoemaker, S., *Identity, Cause, and Mind*, Cambridge University Press, Cambridge, 1984, pp.234-260.

Shoemaker, S. (1984), 'Personal Identity. A Materialist's Account', in Shoemaker, S. and Swinburne, R., *Personal Identity*, Basil Blackwell, Oxford, pp.67-132.

Shoemaker, S. (1986), 'Introspection and the Self', in Shoemaker, S., *The First-Person Perspective and Other Essays*, Cambridge University Press, Cambridge, 1996, pp.3-24.

Sim, S. (2000), *Contemporary Continental Philosophy. The New Scepticism*, Ashgate, Aldershot.

Smith, A. (1759), *The Theory of Moral Sentiments*, Raphael, D.D. and Macfie, A.L. (eds), Oxford University Press, Oxford, 1976.

Snowdon, P.F. (1990), 'Persons, Animals, and Ourselves', in Gill, Ch. (ed.), *The Person and the Human Mind. Issues in Ancient and Modern Philosophy*, Clarendon Press, Oxford, pp.83-107.

Sontag, S. (1979), 'The Dummy', in Sontag, S., *I, etcetera*, Vintage Books, New York, pp.85-97.

Stevenson, L. and Haberman, D.L. (1998), *Ten Theories of Human Nature. Third Edition*, University Press, Oxford.

Strawson, P.F. (1959), *Individuals. An Essay in Descriptive Metaphysics*, Methuen, London.

Strawson, P.F. (1962), 'Freedom and Resentment', in Strawson, P.F., *Freedom and Resentment and Other Essays*, Methuen, London, 1974, pp.1-25.

Strawson, P.F. (1966), 'Self, Mind and Body', in Strawson, P.F., *Freedom and Resentment and Other Essays*, Methuen, London, 1974, pp.169-177.

Strawson, P.F. (1976), 'Entity and Identity', in Lewis, H.D. (ed.), *Contemporary British Philosophy, Fourth Series*, Allen and Unwin, London, pp.193-220.

Strawson, P.F. (1980), 'P.F. Strawson Replies', in Van Straaten, Z. (ed.), *Philosophical Subjects. Essays Presented to P.F. Strawson*, Clarendon Press, Oxford, pp.260-296.

Strawson, P.F. (1985), *Skepticism and Naturalism: Some Varieties. The Woodbridge Lectures 1983*, Columbia University Press, New York.

Swinburne, R. (1973/74), 'Personal Identity', *Proceedings of the Aristotelian Society*, vol. LXXIV, pp.231-247.

Swinburne, R. (1984), 'Personal Identity. The Dualist Theory', in Shoemaker, S. and Swinburne, R., *Personal Identity*, Basil Blackwell, Oxford, pp.1-66.

Swinburne, R. (1986), *The Evolution of the Soul*, Clarendon Press, Oxford.

Taylor, C. (1977), 'What is Human Agency?', in Taylor, C., *Human Agency and Language. Philosophical Papers I*, Cambridge University Press, Cambridge, 1985, pp.15-44.

Taylor, C. (1989), *Sources of the Self. The Making of the Modern Identity*, Cambridge University Press, Cambridge.

Taylor, C. (1991), *The Ethics of Authenticity*. Harvard University Press, Cambridge, Massachusetts.

Taylor, G. (1985), *Pride, Shame, and Guilt. Emotions of Self-Assessment*, Clarendon Press, Oxford.

Thalberg, I. (1978), 'Hierarchical Analyses of Unfree Action', *Canadian Journal of Philosophy*, vol. 8, pp.211-226.

Thomson, J.J. (1997), 'People and their Bodies', in Dancy, J. (ed.) *Reading Parfit*, Blackwell, Oxford, pp.202-229.

Tooley, M. (1986), 'Abortion and Infanticide', in Singer, P. (ed.), *Applied Ethics*, Oxford University Press, Oxford, pp.57-85.

Tugendhat, E. (1986), *Self-Consciousness and Self-Determination*, Stern, P. (transl.), The MIT Press, Cambridge, Massachusetts.

Velleman, J.D. (1992), 'What Happens When Someone Acts?', *Mind*, vol. 101, pp.461-480.

Watson, G. (1975), 'Free Agency', in Watson, G. (ed.), *Free will*, Oxford University Press, Oxford, 1982, pp.96-110.

Watson, G. (1987), 'Free Action and Free Will', *Mind*, vol. 96, pp.145-172.

Wiggins, D. (1967), *Identity and Spatio-temporal Continuity*, Basil Blackwell, Oxford.

Wiggins, D. (1980), *Sameness and Substance*, Basil Blackwell, Oxford.

Wiggins, D. (1987), 'The Person as Object of Science, as Subject of Experience, and as Locus of Value', in Peacocke, A. and Gillett, G. (eds), *Persons and Personality. A Contemporary Inquiry*, Basil Blackwell, Oxford, pp.56-74.

Williams, B. (1956/57), 'Personal Identity and Individuation', in Williams, B, *Problems of the Self*, Cambridge University Press, Cambridge, 1973, pp.1-18.

Williams, B. (1966), 'Imagination and the Self', in Williams, B, *Problems of the Self*, Cambridge University Press, Cambridge, 1973, pp.26-45.

Williams, B. (1973), *Problems of the Self*, Cambridge University Press, Cambridge.

Williams, B. (1976), 'Persons, Character and Morality', in Oksenberg Rorty, A. (ed.), *The Identities of Persons*, University of California Press, Berkeley.

Wittgenstein, L. (1922), *Tractatus Logico-Philosophicus*, D. Pears and B.F. McGuinness (transl.), Routledge and Kegan Paul, London.

Wittgenstein, L. (1953), *Philosophical Investigations / Philosophische Untersuchungen*, G.E.M. Anscombe (transl.), Basil Blackwell, Oxford.

Wittgenstein, L. (1958), *The Blue and Brown Books*, Basil Blackwell, Oxford.

Wittgenstein, L. (1967), *Zettel*, G.E.M. Anscombe and G.H. von Wright (eds), G.E.M. Anscombe (transl.), Basil Blackwell, Oxford.

Wittgenstein, L. (1980), *Culture and Value / Vermischte Bemerkungen*, G.H. von Wright (ed.), P. Winch (transl.), Basil Blackwell, Oxford.

Wolf, S. (1987), 'Sanity and the Metaphysics of Responsibility', in Christman, J. (ed.), *The Inner Citadel. Essays on Individual Autonomy*, Oxford University Press, Oxford, pp.137-151.

Wolf, S. (1990), *Freedom Within Reason*, Oxford University Press, Oxford.

Wollheim, R. (1979), 'Memory, Experiental Memory, and Personal Identity', in MacDonald, G.F. (ed.), *Perception and Identity. Essays Presented to A.J. Ayer with his Replies to them*, Macmillan, London, pp.186-234.

Zemach, E.M. (1970), 'The Unity and Indivisibility of the Self', *International Philosophical Quarterly*, vol. X, pp.542-555.

Index of Names

Albritton 109
Aristotle 4, 105
Barthes 4
Benjamin 4
Berkeley 4
Boethius 17
Butler 15, 26, 59, 153

Chisholm 9, 15
Coburn 57
Cooley 102, 142

Davidson 78
Dennett 87
Derrida 4 - 5
Descartes 15, 17, 59, 61
Dworkin 10, 88 - 91, 104, 107

Elster 101

Fichte 4
Foucault 4
Frankfurt 10, 88 - 90, 92 - 93, 95, 97 -
    99, 104, 107 - 120, 122, 124 - 125,
    129, 131, 134 - 135, 146
Freud 5 - 6

Gadamer 4

Habermas 4
Hegel 4, 6
Heidegger 2, 4 - 5, 53

Heraclitus 15
Hobbes 4, 108, 111, 113
Hume 4, 15, 26, 33, 59, 61, 63, 66
Husserl 4

Irigaray 4

James 102

Kant 4

Lacan 4
Leibniz 18, 26, 31
Levinas 5
Lichtenberg 39
Locke 4, 15, 20, 22, 59, 151 - 152
Lyotard 4 - 5

MacIntyre 80
Mackie 23
Madell 15, 59
Malcolm 135
Marx 5 - 6
Mauss 16 - 17
McIntyre 148
McTaggart 59, 61
Mead 103, 141, 145
Merleau-Ponty 4

Nagel 135
Nietzsche 5 - 6
Nussbaum 105

Parfit 9, 15, 37, 55, 59, 134
Perry 9, 37, 49, 55
Plato 4, 88, 105

Quinton 9, 15

Reid 15, 31, 59, 116 - 117, 157 - 158
Ricoeur 4
Rorty 148
Russell 4, 18, 59, 61 - 62
Ryle 4

Sartre 4
Schelling 4

Shoemaker 9, 15, 66
Smith 101
Strawson 7, 9, 18, 58, 67 - 71, 73 - 75, 78, 85 - 87
Swinburne 9, 15

Taylor 11, 131, 134, 139 - 141, 143 - 149
Taylor, Gabriele 104

Watson 98, 137
Wiggins 75 - 76
Williams 76
Wittgenstein 6, 64, 70, 131 - 135, 137 - 138, 141, 144 - 145

For Product Safety Concerns and Information please contact our EU
representative GPSR@taylorandfrancis.com
Taylor & Francis Verlag GmbH, Kaufingerstraße 24, 80331 München, Germany